Letters to Dolcidia

Letters to Dolcidia

(1954–1983)

edited by
Gian Carlo Sibilia

translated by
Michael J. Smith

ORBIS BOOKS

Maryknoll, New York 10545

Originally published in Italian as *Lettere a Dolcidia*
by Cittadella Editrice, Assisi, Italy in 1989
Copyright © Cittadella Editrice, 1989

This English translation first published in Great Britain in
1991 by Fount Paperbacks, an imprint of
HarperCollins*Religious*, 77–85 Fulham Palace Road,
London W6 8JB

Published in the United States of America by Orbis Books,
Maryknoll NY 10545

Copyright in the English translation by
HarperCollins*Publishers* © 1991

Printed in Great Britain by HarperCollins Manufacturing, Glasgow

Library of Congress Cataloging-in-Publication Data

Carretto, Carlo.
    [Lettere a Dolcidia. English]
    Letters to Dolcidia: 1954–1983/by Carlo Carretto; edited by
Gian Carlo Sibilia; translated by Michael J. Smith.
        p.   cm.
    Translation of: Lettere a Dolcidia.
    ISBN 0–88344–720–7 (pbk.): $9.95
    1. Carretto, Carlo—Correspondence.   2. Carretto, Dolcidia,
1908–1986—Correspondence.   3. Little Brothers of Jesus—Italy—
Correspondence.   4. Nuns—Italy—Correspondence.   I. Carretto,
Dolcidia, 1908–1986.   II. Sibilia, Gian Carlo, 1934–   .
III. Title.
BX4705.C3183A4   1991
271'.79—dc20   91–28836
    [B]   CIP

Contents

Foreword

These letters are published just as they were written; only occasionally have capital letters, punctuation, transcriptions and dates been edited; very rarely I have put into square brackets references which should be regarded as confidential for the time being. The few Scripture quotations, which often follow the sense rather than the text, have been left as found.

I have had opportunity in the notes to fill out the background of the Brotherhood of Charles de Foucauld, the spiritual family which marked Carlo Carretto so strongly.

Since this volume is the first in a series aimed at a complete biography, the notes may open up some new lines of research on this little brother of the Gospel.

The manuscripts reproduced here, like others in the process of publication, form part of the Carretto/Jesus Caritas Foundation at the Abbey of Sassovivo in Foligno (Perugia). I would like to invite anyone in possession of writings by or about Carlo Carretto to let me know about them.

I would like to thank the Carretto and Turchi families for the freedom given me to publish this collection of letters, and the Little Brothers Leonardo de Mola and Paolo Onori for their collaboration.

Gian Carlo Sibilia

Gian Carlo Sibilia was born at Tripoli in Libya in 1934, and is now the Rome director of GIAC, involved in serving the Church in Italy and abroad. His studies and professional activities gave him a background in the business world, and in 1970 he became a priest of the Church in Foligno (Perugia), where he carries out various tasks.

He is the Founder and Prior of the Little Brothers and Little Sisters of the 'Jesus Caritas Community', and is in charge of the spiritual magazine of the 'Charles de Foucauld Family'.

For more than twenty-five years he was a close friend of Carlo Carretto, who entrusted the sorting out of his writings to him: letters, spiritual diaries . . . that is to say, whatever was left after they had made a selection together, which they did several times in recent years. On these occasions, by Carlo's own express wish, the bulk of his manuscripts were burned.

Biographical Notes on Carlo Carretto

Carlo Carretto was born in Alessandria (Piedmont) on April 2nd 1910 to a family of farm labourers from the Langhe; he was the third of six children, of whom four entered religious life. After a brief stay in Alessandria, the family moved to a suburb of Turin, where there was a Salesian oratory which had a great influence on Carlo and his whole family. At the age of eighteen Carlo was at Gattinara as a primary school teacher. He took an active part in the Turin Catholic Action for Youth, which he entered at the age of twenty-three at the invitation of Luigi Gedda, who was its president. He read for degrees in history and philosophy while continuing to teach in primary school, first at Sommariva Bosco and then in Turin. In 1940 he was awarded promotion to headmaster, and was appointed as such to Bono (Sardinia). Shortly afterwards he was relieved of his post, following disputes with the fascist regime, arising from the nature of his teaching and the influence it exercised even outside school hours. He was held under guard in Isili, then sent back to Piedmont. Here he was allowed to take up a position as headmaster again in

Condove. During the period of the Salo Republic he was asked by Rome to support the ranks of Catholic Action in Northern Italy. Since he did not pledge himself to the Salò Republic, he was struck off the board of headmasters and kept under surveillance. In 1945 he was summoned to Rome by Pope Pius XII and Luigi Gedda to organize the National Association of Catholic Teachers. In 1946 he became president of Italian Catholic Youth Action (GIAC – Gioventù Italiana di Azione Cattolica) and shortly afterwards founded the Bureau International de la Jeunesse Catholique, of which he became vice-president. In 1948, on the occasion of the 80th anniversary of Catholic Action, he organized a big rally of young people in Rome, the famous 'green berets' rally. In 1953, the tensions which had been simmering in Catholic circles about relations with politics broke out into the open. Carlo found himself at odds with an important wing of Catholic opinion which favoured an alliance with the Italian Right, and he had to resign as a president of Catholic Action, and with Lazzati, La Pira, Gonella and others look for new paths along which to direct committed lay Catholic activity. It was in this period of hard and painful searching that he reached his decision to become a member of the religious congregation of Father Charles de Foucauld's Little Brothers of Jesus. And so he left for Algeria to enter the novitiate on December 8th 1954. For ten years he led the life of a hermit in the Sahara, where he had a deep experience of the interior life and of prayer, in silence and in work, an experience which he communicated in the book which was to become a bestseller, *Letters from the Desert*, and in all the books he was to write afterwards. This experience was to nourish the rest of his life and later activity.

When he returned to Europe he spent periods with communities of Little Brothers in Turkey, France and Italy. In 1965, he went to Spello (Perugia), where a community of Little Brothers had recently sprung up in a disused ancient monastery. He was appointed by his superiors to be in charge of the community, which was originally opened for members of the congregation to come and spend a period of time as hermits. But Carlo's spirit of initiative and the prestige he enjoyed very quickly opened up the community to welcome anyone, believer or not, who wished to spend a period reflecting and searching for faith in prayer, manual labour and the exchange of experiences. Little by little, many country cottages on the surrounding hills, scattered over an area of several kilometres, were added to the site of the community's monastery; they became known as 'hills of hope' and were loaned by the farmers who owned them for the use of the Little Brothers, who turned each of them into a hermitage. This increased the numbers who could share in the community without reducing the spirit of recollection and prayer which was the hallmark of time spent at Spello, because the hermitages were separated by a distance from one another. For twenty years, Carretto was to be the tireless animator of this centre, well-known both in Italy and abroad. During these years he took up again his activities as a writer, which he had begun during his youth but which had been interrupted during his desert years. Of his early books, it is worth recalling *Made in Heaven* (1945), which aroused controversy in

Catholic circles because some of its ideas were ahead of their time.

As a master of the spoken and written word, Carlo Carretto used both to great effect to communicate to others his 'discoveries' and his experience of the faith. His books have been translated into many languages and have gained him a legion of readers and friends from every country, and he received frequent invitations to give lectures and address spiritual meetings all over the world. His deeply inward spirituality did not cut him off from the world and its problems, but rather drove him to get involved with it in a spirit of service, as is shown by his numerous contributions in articles to important Italian newspapers and magazines at crucial points in the national political or religious life.

On October 4th 1988, the feast of Saint Francis, after some years' illness, in his little cell at Spello he completed his journey towards Eternity in an atmosphere of great Easter joy shared by hundreds of people from every corner of Italy and from abroad.

Who was Dolcidia?

Dolcidia Carretto, Carlo's sister, was born in Camerano (Cuneo) on November 1st 1908. Along with her sister Emerenziana, she had regular Salesian contacts, first in Alessandria and later in Turin, especially the Oratory of the Daughters of Mary Help of Christians in the Borgo San Paolo. After leaving school she worked for a number of years as a bookkeeper before entering the Daughters of Mary Help of Christians, where she made her first vows on August 5th 1936.

She was appointed mistress of the novices and postulants at the mother house on the Via Cumiana in Turin, where she was remembered as a hardworking woman with special gifts of kindness and understanding towards young girls. In 1938 she was appointed secretary to Mother Angela Vespa, who held various posts in the Salesian Congregation before becoming mother general.

She worked with Mother Vespa for 31 years, accompanying her on her various travels and giving an example of affectionate and loyal devotion, in a spirit of concern and self-sacrifice.

Whether in Turin or elsewhere, Sister Dolcidia's

day began at 4:30. Its first hours were given over to personal and community prayer.

Anyone who invited her to take a little rest received the same reply: 'If I don't pray a bit early in the morning, I've no other time during the day: there's a lot of work to be done and I should give the Lord the best.'

Mother Angela recognized and appreciated her secretary's work and devotion. In the final years of her life she let it be known to her sister, Sister Emerenziana, in these words, 'Your sister, Sister Dolcidia, was always loyal to me.' Yet her highly confidential work did not prevent her from being kind, welcoming and attentive to other 'sisters' with whom she came into contact in the course of her duties.

After the death of Mother Angela she was appointed secretary to the Central Provincial, Mother Pierina Magnani. There followed another twelve years of office work which she once more carried out with zeal, prudence and precision.

Next came a period of her life given over to raising funds for her missionary brother in Thailand.

On December 8th 1982, Sister Dolcidia began a slow and painful journey towards heaven. A relentless illness confined her to her little room, and she coped with her deteriorating health very philosophically.

One day she said to her sister, Sister Emerenziana, who had come to visit her, 'I don't know what more the Lord wants from me.'

On October 24th 1985, her brother Bishop Pietro stopped over in Turin. The superior had an altar laid in her cell, and on three consecutive mornings he celebrated Holy Mass, to the great consolation of Sister Dolcidia.

On the day of his departure he came to see her and they said the Rosary together. The day ended with him blessing the convent and that was his last greeting to her on Earth.

In December she saw her sister Liliana again and her brother-in-law Mario Turchi. A few days later she said, 'I have to have one more meeting with Carlo and then I can and want to go.'

Carlo arrived on January 4th 1986, the day of her death, and they both felt the light touch of God's fatherly presence. Sister Emerenziana was also there and shared her sister's final hours.

According to her account:

Carlo and Dolcidia had always cherished the same ideals and their common care was to love the Lord. A number of Sisters gathered in the cell and he discussed spiritual matters with them.

About 5:00 pm. he said to Sister Dolcidia, 'You have a great desire for Heaven. Jesus used to pray in Aramaic; this was his language, the language of his people. Let us hold our rosaries and repeat the prayer "Maranatha" (Come, Lord Jesus!).' At the end of the Rosary he said, 'Now I leave you my kiss; may it be a sign of life or death according to God's will.' He said goodbye and departed.

At 8:30 pm. Sister Dolcidia entered heaven, on the first Sunday of the year 1986, the day before the vigil of the Epiphany.

The Letters

1

My dearest Sister,

I'm writing to you because *I know you're very concerned* and because I think I'll catch you at this very moment in church, praying for your brother who's going away.

Poor Dolce![2] The Lord has given you the vocation of holding in your heart all the cares of the family. And of suffering them.

Don't worry, Dolce; it's God who's calling me. I know His voice. Think of my life up till now: I've always followed the right star, haven't I? Haven't I pulled in great netfuls of souls? But I couldn't rest on my laurels any more: my capital was all used up. I would have ended up a mediocre representative for God, dissatisfied with myself. There was nothing for it but to make a break, and since God said 'come', I had the courage (by his grace) to respond.

Just think: I'm sailing the same African sea as St Augustine: over there is his diocese of Hippo.

I'm going into the *desert*, my desert. Even if I'm making a mistake and have to return (but I don't think so), I can't imagine anything better than a year's *desert*, real desert. I want to empty myself and become nothing, then say to Jesus: fill me with Yourself alone.

Isn't that a grace? Be happy. You know I've always been shrewd and made good deals. I've never made such a good deal as this.

How often we have discussed the sterility of today's apostolate. I want to go and study the real thing, because this is the best situation and the best place to understand how useless the superstructures are.

And after all, you will pray for me: You won't abandon me to my loneliness, will you?

I'm so happy, Dolce! I feel as though I'm 15 and just starting out. It will be the sweetest novitiate of my life, made in the place where the Desert Fathers made theirs, in the biblical footsteps of the real mystics of the past, those who laid the foundations of European Christianity.

What an immense grace God is giving me! But how did I come to deserve it after so many sins? Truly our God is a God of mercy! He loads you with gifts at the very time you're giving Him no thought, or worse, betraying Him.

He is Father!

And I want to become His son, His real son.

He is Jesus my brother.

And I want to become a genuine brother to Him.

He is the Spirit of Love.

And I want to enrol in His School of Fire and let myself be all burnt up.

What a joy, my dear sister!

I send you such a hug as I've never given you in my life, because I love you as never before.

Love, Carlo

2

El Abiodh,[1] December 16th 1954

Dearest Dolce, dearest all,

Here I am settled in the peace of the African desert. Today dawn broke on my first morning as a novice after a night under the stars.

Let's go back and tell the story in the right order. As you well know, I left Termini on the evening of the Immaculate Conception after a quiet night, and reached Marseilles with Poldo and Nino[2] in pouring rain. We soon reached the local brotherhood where they were expecting us. We spent that evening and the whole of the following day visiting the French brotherhood about which Nino will have already spoken. In the meantime, I booked a place on the ferry to continue my journey as soon as possible, while Nino and Poldo worked out their return to Italy.

On the morning of the 11th I went aboard the Bel-Abbes, a ferry of almost 10,000 tons, after saying goodbye to the friends who had come with me. The crossing was good despite a rather choppy sea and . . . headlong dashes by some of the passengers, especially the ladies. A day later, or to be exact at one o'clock on Sunday 12th, I set foot on African soil at the port of Orano. Here too I was expected, and spent Sunday afternoon at Mass in the Cathedral and visiting this beautiful African city. On Monday morning I journeyed on southwards in a coach bound for Jaida, passing through the fertile Algerian coastal strip.

It was wonderful arable land, just as well cultivated

as the most fertile lands of Europe. Vines, olives, fruit trees, oranges, mandarins, wheat: everything which a Mediterranean country can produce. And the early Spring vegetables like peas and so on were fully ripe.

After Jaida I took another coach for Geryville, the first leg of my long journey. Here, little by little as I moved on, the vines decreased and the rocks and cold increased, a sure sign that the sea's kindly influence was falling behind me. I arrived at Geryville in the afternoon as guest of the White Fathers,[3] where I was received, as everywhere, with much warmth. I spent the night in Geryville with . . . a stove burning in my room (this tells you that the Sahara is a very cold land which gets hot when the sun shines). In the morning I was lucky enough to find the sun shining so that I could leave again for the South (when it rains, and in winter it rains a lot in this first stretch of steppe, nobody leaves because the tracks are flooded with water and impossible to travel). So I set off in a sturdy truck, with which to tackle the hardest 60-odd miles (after the 250 already travelled).

Bear it in mind that it took me almost six hours, seeing that we had to travel very very slowly along impossible tracks through the steppe. The steppe isn't yet desert, but a preparation for it. Imagine a vast plateau at more than 3000 feet strewn with rocks, sand, clumps of grass as tough as steel blades and here and there nomad Bedouins' herds of sheep and camels.

Towards the end of the journey the steppe stopped and the real desert began. In fact, El Abiodh is the last centre of habitation before the wide open Sahara, a real sea of sand with just a few oases where water bubbles up.

I arrived at 3:00 pm. to be met with great eagerness by about 40 French, Belgian, Peruvian, Spanish and Canadian novices (just about the whole world in fact), and particularly by Fr Paoli,[4] who was here, dressed as a novice.

El Abiodh is a tiny but very beautiful oasis. It consists of an Arab-style building which includes a church and some porticoes, off which open the cells. A community of about 50 Little Brothers lives here, dedicating themselves to manual labour and prayer. They make bread and till the fields (the few possible), build walls, make household objects and live as the poorest of the poor.

All possessions are held in common and there are no aesthetic considerations (I've still got things to learn). We eat sitting on the floor in the dining-room off a single aluminium plate. We drink water out of the one jug and anyone who is squeamish can leave within the day. In the cells we sleep on the floor (there are no beds) and everything is reduced to the indispensable minimum.

The whole thing recalls the original Franciscans, but the local atmosphere is an Arab one of the greatest simplicity possible to imagine. It really is a complete stripping away! And it is just this which leads to the most complete feeling of freedom and joy. Around me I see nothing but happy faces oozing joy at every pore.

They are Spartans in training for a really hard life. This is our timetable: rise at 3:00 for prayers until 7:00.

Begin work at 7:00 which lasts until 13:00. Builders,

farm-workers, carpenters, electricians, truck-drivers etc. They work on the house, they build the women's novitiate a few hundred yards away and they make all the craft objects for the surrounding Arab villages. In the afternoon, adoration of the Blessed Sacrament, study and a bit more work.

At 9:00 we go off to sleep or to write letters. After 11:00 we all have to be in our beds, which are not beds, because we sleep on the floor on a mat. The nights are as cold as in our mountains, and the days are hot. The same thing happens here as in our mountains, where there is an extraordinary difference between when the sun is shining and when it's not. We go from a few degrees Centigrade below zero to 30 above. They say that in summer it goes from a few degrees above zero to 43 above in the sun.

We shall see. At the moment it's winter and comfortable.

I have been given a cell on my own, which is seen as a mark of respect, but I don't think it will last long because novices continue to arrive and there's no more space.

I have fallen in with some amazing people. They are all used to tough spiritual battles and, like us, have made headway in them. No young person is taken on before the age of twenty and I think I understand the reason. You and Emerenziana,[5] who did ordinary novitiates, have no idea of what things are like here. Nobody thinks about material things. There is almost a couldn't-care-less attitude towards all comfort and a search for austerity.

But it's all about prayer and the hours of adoration feel like communal battles. *The silence is infinite* and the desert which surrounds this oasis is forever inviting us to keep quiet. This is really the most solemn impression I have had since my arrival.

I don't yet know what I shall be doing: perhaps they will make me a builder or a field-worker because I am sturdy. It is the Trappist rule: 7 hours work, 7 hours prayer, and seven or less of sleep.

You can imagine how happy I feel! Really happy! I've received an infinite grace from the Lord and I've got to be worthy of it. Don't worry. I wrote to you, Dolcidia, *that I have always found my guiding star. I feel I've found it this time too.*

God loves me like a baby and is guiding me like a child. Don't worry. *Instead pray for me as much as you can.*

I'm getting Lili to act as my secretary and type up copies of this letter and the others I shall send for our sisters and Piero. I can't spend time writing the same things to everybody.

I'll tell you what to do about my friends when the time is right.

Be happy and . . . Happy Christmas! I don't know whether another letter will reach you beforehand: in any case, *save me a place* next to you in the dining-room. I willingly offer up the pain of being away for Papà and Mamma.

Lots of kisses, Carlo

3

El Abiodh-Sidi-Sheikh, Christmas 1954

Dearest Dolcidia, dearest all,

The Christmas star of 1954 has led me into the great Sahara desert in the footsteps of Fr de Foucauld.[1]

El Abiodh, which is where I am living at the moment, is a tiny oasis perched on the edge of the great sea of sand, which stretches south as far as Equatorial Africa. It is made up of two little Arab villages built out of sun-dried brick, in which the population lives barricaded around a few wells, committed to tending herds and cultivating a few little fields of corn. Next to the two villages stands the Novitiate of the 'Little Brothers of Jesus',[2] of which Fr de Foucauld dreamed and for which he wrote the Rule; Fr Voillaume,[3] the author of the book *Seeds of the Desert*[4] organized it with a few companions.

The first thing which strikes you when you come to El Abiodh is the silence. It is an immense, total, all-absorbing silence. The last 62 miles of steppe, over a poor road even for trucks, are a good preparation for this African setting of stark horizons, nomad herdsmen and sand battling against the last clumps of grass and thorns.

It would certainly be difficult to find a place more suited to meditation and adoration, and we can see at once why Fr de Foucauld, who was called the last Desert Father, said this place had a particular power to call distracted and sensual souls back to God.

The nomads' black tents (symbol of the human journey towards the Eternal Pastures), the Arabs prostrate in prayer, the luminosity of the sky (European eyes are not used to this), the great sea of sand which surrounds us, the inescapable realities of silence and death – these are indisputably the elements of an ascetical life. In this place the Novice master's invitation seems natural: divest yourself totally of all you had until yesterday – clothes, suitcases, boxes, nips of drinks, dabs of scent, hidden comforts – while you repeat to yourself: *Take no more care for your life and health than for a tree or a falling leaf.*

Once stripped naked you are reclothed in workman's clothes which are not your own, and a white Arab 'gandura' which you will use in church during choir. That is the way your life begins, as a pupil of a Desert Father.

You get a mat on the ground, a sleeping-bag into which you climb on cold nights, a pair of sandals and a Rule specially designed to bend the stiffest backs like mine. It could be summed up more or less as: 7 hours' manual labour, 7 hours' prayer and 7 hours' sleep.

This is what is needed for this band of forty French, Belgian, African, Chilean, Spanish and Brazilian novices. They have all, like me, reached adulthood, been tested in battle and infected by the 'problematic' and by 'cultural indoctrination' of a religious sort. Here the overriding law is: 'Stop thinking about what you have to do to win over the Brothers, worry about *being*. From now on your sermon has to be your life and not your words. And living an authentic *life* means copying the life of Jesus.'

Fr Foucauld was fond of distinguishing three periods in the life of Jesus: Nazareth, the desert and the public life.

He lived out his Rule on this scheme: To copy

Nazareth, seek out solitude to fill yourself with God, burn with love for souls.

1) Nazareth. To achieve the imitation of Jesus of Nazareth, you accept being poor labourers for the whole of your life. This is a major effort, especially for those of us who come from the middle class. The set-up of the Novitiate, and of the Brotherhood where we will go to live later, is based on work. The vow of poverty accepts the same poverty as labourers and wage-earners, in a word the people. Moreover, it was the poverty of Jesus.

Before clothing me in the Novice's habit, Fr Voillaume asked me, 'Are you ready for the Gospel of Jesus, not only to live the life of a poor man with no possessions, but also to accept the conditions of the poor, who must work to live, as divine law requires?'

Once this premise has been stated, the rest falls into place. Would you like me to give you an idea of how we live? Imagine a building site along a road under construction. Clothes, food, medicine, conveniences: they are exactly the same as those imposed by the harsh law of manual labour which is the labour of the poorest. There is food and enough of it, but it comes in a mess tin with no refinements. And if you leave any, you eat it in the evening, and if you still leave some, you eat it the next day; that's what the poor do. Clothes? As tattered and dusty as on a building site. The infirmary? If you saw it, and its infirmarian, you would understand what I meant before by the saying, 'Don't be more anxious about your own life than about a tree or a falling leaf.'

2) *The desert.* This is certainly one of the marks of the team which I have joined by becoming a 'Little Brother'. Here they are so convinced that the reasons

for the 'crisis' are within ourselves, in our superficiality, in the very superstructures of our piety, that they adopt no half-measures to get away from it. They have to make a clean sweep, and then with the one book they let you keep, the Bible, they send you out into the solitude and give the desert the job of getting to work on you.

It has to be experienced to be believed, so much so that I've been convinced right from my first encounter that the Lord created the desert just to give space to souls needing to collect themselves. That is why, faced with the dominant paganism of the early centuries, Christianity went to sink its roots in the desert, with the monasticism of East and West.

3) *The apostolic life*. The apostolate of the Little Brothers is directed towards the poor and most forsaken, or better still towards those furthest from Christ, where words are almost useless but witness is necessary. That is why the two great areas towards which we are urged are Islam and the world of work.

What do you preach to a Muslim? It's not just useless, it's impossible. What do you preach to workers poisoned by Marxism? It's the same.

What then? You stand alongside them, living as they do, with the witness of a Christian life rich in love and joy despite the pain of labour. When it's necessary one should talk too, but the overriding concern is to demonstrate the goodness of the Gospel with one's life.

You can see the power of this formula, which at any rate is the one which has won me over.

You can see why we study Arabic here, and Russian even more so. You have your finger on the pulse of our situation, the situation towards which the

modern world is moving, so you won't find it difficult to see the fruitfulness of such an evangelical
appeal, launched by a poor hermit in love with God
and mankind, such as was Charles de Foucauld.

That is why he left the Trappists.

He saw them to be too removed from people. He
reconstituted them on a smaller scale alongside
people. He wanted his followers to be Trappists in
the midst of the suffering, the poverty and the
insecurity of the poor of our day. He wanted their
sole concern to be the love of Christ made present
in 'permanent prayer' and continual 'availability' to
people.

But let's leave these things which I put badly and
which you can find put well in the book *Seeds of the
Desert*. Let's deal with simpler things which I, your
brother and friend, can tell you.

To start with, I can tell you that I remember you all.
In the long periods of adoration before the Blessed
Sacrament – there is always Exposition here after
work – your faces and your problems pass one by
one through my mind. It is so easy here to remember
everybody.

Then I can tell you again that I will pray for you
and I shall be happy if you will entrust me with this
task, especially for the things that are hardest and
most burdensome for you. In this way I shall feel
that I am battling alongside you again just as I used
to do.

Forgive me for writing this communal letter. Basically it was a question of making the same introduc-
tory remarks, and it went against the grain to waste
time repeating them all in a lot of letters.

Later on it won't be like that: it will give me real

pleasure to get down to discussing with you matters which are woven deeply into our friendship, and our ideals of love for God and his Church.

Pray for me that I will be faithful to the call of Jesus – imperious as it was – so that I may achieve a life of effective evangelical witness and make up for such a dull and bombastic past.

I carry you with me in all love in my God-filled solitude.

Love, Carlo

4

El Abiodh, January 21st 1955

Dearest Dolce and dear all,

First things first: *I'm happy, happy, happy and I feel like I'm 15 years old*.

I got the feeling from Sr Dolcidia's letter that you all (or she) were rather taken aback by the harshness of the life which we lead here. NO, don't worry yourselves in the slightest but believe me genuinely and literally when I say: *I'm happy*. It's true that life here is as tough as it is for those in the mountains, but what does toughness matter? Mountain people enjoy it even when they sleep on a plank floor and eat out of a mess tin, don't they?

The life we lead is Spartan: sleeping on the floor and wearing permanently dirty overalls and not bothering with a tie don't matter . . . but the whole thing is accepted in such a carefree spirit of joy *that we feel sorry for those who peer into the mirror and worry about*

the colour of their shirt. The fact is that here we go
back to school *to become poor*, and you know that
poverty is apparently painful but really nothing less
than a beatitude (blessed are the poor) and therefore
a source of great, very great joy. What is more, it is
a school for *freedom* and *detachment*, both of them
divine and marvellous things.

Mamma, don't you worry about what I'm eating:
I'm eating very well. To be sure, if you served at
home some of the dishes served here . . . you would
hear shrieks and see long faces. Of course there are
things to laugh about. The most unthinkable things
come out of the kitchen and we have the strangest
possible menus. Imagine this for a lunch: starter:
soup; main course: pasta; dessert: dates; or another:
first course: boiled potatoes; main course: mashed
potatoes; dessert: figs.

Now they want me to join the kitchen; I'm sure
that even if I prepared the food with my feet I would
be a hit. But this doesn't matter, and if I make the
pasta too tasty they'll chase me out of the kitchen as
a *tempter*.

You see, here we live like real workmen because
we have to pick up our trade from the teaching of
Jesus of Nazareth. But I wouldn't have believed that
I would find so much joy in freeing myself from so
much vanity, superficiality, greed and pretension.

Detachment from things leaves you with such a
sense of *freedom!* You don't worry any more whether
you're ugly or handsome, bearded or beardless. Here
it's rather almost a competition to get into the worst
clothes and get rid of the slavery of middle-class
habits (would you believe that I trim my beard once
a week, I who used to shave every morning?).

Obviously, all this is not a goal, *it's a means* towards eliminating every form of servitude, towards making us sturdy, towards learning to suffer, to work *and to become simple because the Gospel is for the simple* and is better understood that way.

All the complications of modern life, especially a rich one, are full of poison and, as I see more clearly now, they take people away from the Gospel and *make them sad*.

That is the way it is and it is for this very reason that I am so happy. The Lord *guided me well* and brought me to just the right place and here I am experiencing my first spiritual benefits.

It's a pity that the time flies so quickly and already more than a month has gone by. I shall have to speed up because I've only a year of testing and then I shall have to leave the desert and go back amongst people. A year is so little for backs as stiff as mine.

A few days ago I left the building-site and became a farmer. I work with cabbages, potatoes and salad vegetables. I've harvested the olives and now I'm pickling them (5 quintals of olives entrusted to my skills). It's rather like the kitchen being entrusted to certain cooks who come out with soup for starters and pasta as a main course.

The weather is fine but very windy. If you could see the desert when the wind blows! You live in a cloud of sand: you breathe sand, you eat sand, your eyes are full of sand. But we also live here because sand is clean, not dirty. When they do not have water, the Arabs purify themselves before prayer by rubbing their hands and faces with sand; they think of it as water. I've haven't yet got that far, but I'm getting there. A few days ago we had a holiday and

I used it to make a 20-mile walk into the desert. I climbed a little mountain from which the whole breadth of the Sahara can be seen. It was marvellous. Enough for now: I'll tell you the rest another time.

Kisses to Mamma, Papà, Liliana, Sr Emerenziana and Sr Dolcidia; to the others all possible affection and the assurance of my prayers.

Love, Carlo

5

El Abiodh, March 1st 1955

Dearest Sr Dolce and Sr Emerenziana,

You are sad (and I'm pleased *because it is a sign of love*) that I haven't sent another personal word to the two of you. I'm doing so today because I have a little free time, since the blizzard of sand which has battered the desert for the last few days has rather changed our work schedule. At any rate, thank you for your most affectionate letters, accompanied as I feel they were by much impassioned prayer. *How dear and precious is our family, united as it is by the bond of mutual prayer!* I think that it is difficult to escape that fact, and that the weaknesses of one member are immediately supplied by the prayers of another, and one member's crisis by another's eagerness, so that the whole team marches forward with confidence towards its Homeland. Don't you agree?

Have you seen how even Liliana has been shaken, how she has settled down, and how *she has understood* and is fulfilling her vocation? And so we go forward again.

You are waiting for a word from me, and that's certainly not difficult, especially nowadays that we have put on the same habit, the same discipline: religious life. You will surely want to know my impressions, my feelings about it, and so forth.

Here goes: there is nothing more *holy* or more *oppressive*, more *sublime* or more *stupid*, more *constructive* or more *useless* than the religious life. Everything depends on the spirit with which you tackle it.

The Rule? It can be a stairway to Heaven or the most inhuman trap you can imagine. *Now I really understand what Jesus was telling the religious of His time: 'The sinners and the tax-collectors will take their places before you!'* For them the religious life was a trap and it was precisely with that that they killed Jesus. Because remember: the people who killed Jesus were the religious of His time, not the sinners and robbers.

As I was saying, it all depends on the spirit in which it is tackled.

For example, what is poverty, ratified and solemnly confirmed by a vow? It's like all the other virtues: having within ourselves 'the same mind as Jesus, who although His state was divine emptied Himself to assume the condition of a slave, and became . . .'

What can poverty become for the religious when it is taken on with a vow?

The solution to all financial problems, the absence of all worries, that happy calm in which everything is looked after and tomorrow is taken care of by gilt-edged securities in the bank.

That's the trap. What is there left resembling the

drama of Mary and Joseph adrift in a foreign land, *really* poor and worried about where to find a bite of food for Jesus? The same goes for all the rest, and in that rest lies an absolute betrayal of the religious life, the Church and Christ.

Obedience? It can be a total, unconditional, joyous abandonment to our one King and Master: or it can be a school for cowardice and a priori rejection of the thing that costs a man dearest: personal responsibility. Isn't that so?

So, my dear sisters, I put it to you: given that we've got the experience, we've got the willingness to serve God, do we want in the years left to us to serve God here on Earth, to live out our vocation in depth, to make it a stairway to Heaven? Nothing else matters any more and we ought to burn all our boats behind us. There is no going back. Since we have chosen to be poor, let us live like the poor; since we have accepted virginity, let's live like virgins . . . and not just like single people; since we have accepted God, let us renounce the world.

How the desert speaks of these things to me! The desert, you see, is just *sand and Sky. Down below sand which is death, up above a Sky which is brighter than anywhere else.* If only you could see the stars here! How they sparkle! Now I understand why the Arabs have not lost their faith as Europeans have and why many European soldiers who came into contact with Arabs came back to God. It's the school of the desert.

When I have a free day, I take a lump of bread and a walking-stick and go off for the whole day. I travel 12 or so miles completely alone in this immense solitude and that way I'm alone with God. It's called 'khalna' in Arabic and it means: to go into solitude.

Remember that one of the Novitiate tests is to make a month of spiritual exercises like this. We set out and travel about 375 miles (Rome-Turin, more or less) towards Beni-Abbès,[1] the oasis where Fr Foucauld lived and found his vocation. It's the test of completely emptying one's mind, and they say it is startlingly effective in leading one to repentance and pure faith. When the time comes I'll tell you about it.

At the moment I'm still here and I work and sing and pray. Above all do I pray. I would like to achieve real intimacy with God and remove the thick veil which divides us and causes my faith to be still so vague and unsure. The route here is the right one: the Blessed Sacrament is exposed almost all day long and the community gravitates towards it.

There is great insistence here on searching for Jesus as a *personal* bridge to God. Basically it's the mystery of the *Incarnation of the Word*, the mystery which comes right up against us and of which we have to make use.

There's no news of human affairs. The voice of the world does not get this far, it's all silence.

My health is excellent, my spirits calm, absolutely calm. I can't tell you how much I pray for you and . . . if you do as much for me we'll be all right.

I hope (this is for Dolce) that her Roman friend wakes up. She already told me that . . . the floods etc., etc. I wish him a bit of Sahara where floods are impossible!

How nice it would be to see you again. It's strange how love grows here instead of fading away!

A big kiss from your Carlo

6

El Abiodh, March 23rd 1955

My dear little big sister,

I've got here on my desk (which is a chest) a scrap of a letter which you wrote to Lili,[1] *bewailing my silence in most heartfelt terms*, and your mighty missive received today. Thank you for both and still more for the first, which speaks to me of all your . . . truly great and deeply-felt affection – which I don't deserve at all. God gave me a beautiful gift when He gave me you as a sister! From all eternity He had thought of this for you and He put you with us for a precise task which your vocation is unearthing day by day and which we will enjoy up there in all its splendour *as God's thought*.

I have the clear impression that you are living out your vocation well – both your personal one and the one which relates to us – and I thank Heaven a great deal for it. All that is left now is one last leap, which ought to be the clearest and most enlightening of all.

I apologize for not having written to you *personally* for so long. It's easy here for folk like me to lose all sense of time. You're right. Collective letters don't work.

Love is personal and needs personal expression. Dialogue with God is personal too: I-Thou is the model for all dialogues based on love. All that's left is the problem of time, but . . . for my little Dolce everything has to be pushed arrogantly out of the way to write personally.

OK?

I'm happy that you are beginning to understand

the reality of my call: it will make it easier for you to help me in thought and prayer.

It was a sudden blow, out of the blue, but that is right for impulsive and passionate characters like your brother Carlo.

I'll have to take Paradise by storm! I'll make a lot of mistakes, but I'll do it with much *generosity* and love! It's my make-up and I can't change it, I just have to sublimate it.

You ask me how I'm doing. Look, Dolce, the desert and the manual labour make problems simpler for you: that's all there is to it.

Simplifying things, reducing them to the essentials, removing the superstructures (how many of them we've got!), getting down to spiritual childhood.

It's all here. The way of the Little Flower, of St Francis, in short of the Gospel: 'If you do not become like little children you shall not enter into the Kingdom,' and that's not easy for those who have been made complicated by sin. To become little children means *to increase our feeling of God's fatherhood over us*, it means to think and act as little children do towards a father they love. He looks after everything, he resolves everything and so on. When does a little child ever worry about tomorrow? Never: the father takes care of it. Isn't that right, sister?

Another thing you get from the simplification of devotion is *the search for a person* rather than an idea. And this person is Jesus.

Jesus looked for as a person in the Eucharist.

Try it and you will see what a great help it is to think this way.

Your brother wants to tell you so many things, and to be honest he exaggerates. Forgive me!

Be sure however that I do really love you and *distance makes this love keener*.

In reality it also causes a bit of suffering, but that's all right.

Here the programme carries on in the form you already know. For work, I now bake bread. It's very beautiful and it gives me joy to see the golden bread come out of the oven.

For reading matter I'm going through the works of St Teresa.

At Easter I shall write to my friend Saporiti. Who knows what he might decide? I send you a big hug and give you the task of giving my regards to Mother Angela[2] in primis usque etc., etc.

Love, Carlo

7

May 1955

Dear Dolce,

I've gone so far as to slip this sheet to you into a letter to Rev. Mother Angela; it has been sent firstly out of natural affection and secondly . . . in order to give you a little something to be getting on with.

Recently I've reached some really fine conclusions in my dialogues with God and I'll write to you about them soon. For the moment I can tell you only that everything is going ahead well and the development of the Lord's grace is bringing me more and more joy and setting high goals.

Thanks for what you wrote to me: you're always good to me and your affection is a great comfort to me and . . . *it spurs me on*.

I fully understand Papà's position and even before I left I realized that it was the bitterest pain both for me and for him. But God will help us, I am sure, with great consolations, even in our mutual separation. I wrote to him yesterday.

The little bit of something to be getting on with is the following:

Buy for me – *ask Lili for the money* – :

1) *the works of St Catherine* (the letters and dialogues). Perhaps you will find them in one volume, including her life. Take advice from the owner of the bookshop; he is sure to know the most recent editions;

2) *a map of the heavens* (not a supernatural one, one *of the stars* – the supernatural one you can do when you're secretary to some big commission up there). I need it to pick out the chief constellations, since I often have to travel by night. Then again, the stars have a special importance to the Arab herdsmen and it's necessary to know them.

I'm sorry to trouble you, but I didn't ask Moncrivello[1] to do it because I didn't want the books in 7 months' time with the Novitiate over (you're to tell Lili however that I gave you the job because you're naturally close to the bookshop). Thanks and . . . be in touch soon.

Love, Carlo

8

Vigil of Pentecost 1955

My dear, darling, sweetest Sister,

The Little Sister with responsibility for Italy is going to Turin: she is a splendid person and I have requested her to visit your place to hand over this letter and the camera for Liliana and . . . to stay with you a while. You will both benefit from it and I'm pleased. First of all I'm going to ask you to take her to visit *Maria Ausiliatrice and Cottolengo*. I'm taking up some of your time, but this way you get to hear my news first hand from someone I saw as she set off for Italy. All right?

I enclose another letter which I wrote yesterday and which is addressed to [. . .]. Read it and send it on. I don't know whether it will find our Romans up there, if not it will await their arrival.

Thanks for your ever good and affectionate letter. I can feel your prayers and I thank you for them.

I really want to be prepared for this Pentecost in silence, humility and love. I have so much need of those qualities, but I hope, hope, hope. I become happier all the time that I chose a Congregation which has contemplation as its aim, and that I've given my life a complete about-turn. It has been a great gift from God, *perhaps the biggest of my life: I feel it to be so*.

I'll write to you again when there's more time. *I've got lots of things inside me to tell you*.

Keep the old folks happy and if they become too solemn *joke with them*. Also give me your impressions of Lili. Give my regards to Mother Angela, who is always good to me. And you have a big hug.

Carlo

P.S. Thanks for whatever you do for the Little Sister. Give her lunch.

9

El Abiodh, Feast of St Peter 1955

Dearest Dolce,

No matter what you're told, you're still the most faithful secretary in history, and if you behave in the same way towards Mother Angela (congratulations on the fantastic new responsibility) I tell you that you're obviously great and worth something to the Congregation. To redress the balance the other way there is the lackadaisical attitude towards letters of my other sister Liliana, and therefore, taking the pluses with the minuses, on balance I can declare myself still a lucky brother. So thanks for your last letter from Pessione[1] dated the 20th and thanks for all the news you sent me.

I've also received a dear letter from Papà, very nice, which brought home to me all the bitterness of separation. You know how fond I am of him! It's like a knife-blade which digs into you and works away at you with anxiety. But you've lived through these things and perhaps you're still living with them more than me and therefore it's useless to talk to you about them. On these occasions I think of the saying of Jesus. 'You who have left . . .'

In any case, it is necessary that it should be so: it is His will and for our good. The life of the spirit needs this pruning, otherwise it does not build or grow, and above all it does not acquire its freedom. I am so happy that I listened to Jesus in this detachment, that I experienced all its bitterness, that I accepted all its consequences. I just want to live it out in its constructive, fertile and vital fullness. That is, I wouldn't want it to be just: 'he's gone a long way away', it's too little and says hardly anything, but: 'he's gone to search for God'. For God, you know, is such a long way away even though he is so close, and the search for him is never over. And yet this search is the one real, precious, and valuable activity to which we are called down here. The rest is a corollary, even the construction of empires, even the most gigantic missionary works. This is what struck me, Dolcidia, when I was thinking about leaving Rome and my old work.

You see, I've done a lot of work for the Church – I'm aware of it. It has been my only thought, my only care. I have raced hard and covered as many miles as the most committed missionary. At a certain point it occurred to me that what the Church lacked was not work, activity, the building of projects or a commitment to bring in souls. What was missing, *or at least was scarce, was the element of prayer, meditation, self-giving, intimacy with God, fidelity to the Holy Spirit and the conviction that He was the real builder of the Church:* in a word, the supernatural element. Let me make myself clear: people of action are needed in the Church but we have to be very careful that their action *does not smother the more delicate but much more important element of prayer*.

If action is missing and there is prayer, the Church lives on, it keeps on breathing, but if prayer is missing and there is only action, the Church withers and dies. Let me give you a physical example from the desert under my nose (the desert is a great teacher!). Imagine a stretch of desert which is all dead sand, at most a few thorns. People decide to transform this desert into a blooming oasis. They set to work. They build roads, side streets, canals, bridges, houses, etc., etc. Nothing changes: *it's all still desert*. The basic element is missing: water. Now anyone who had understood this (it's strange how well we understand the physical world and how little we understand the supernatural) would begin work not *on the surface* but would set about digging deep. They would look for water. They would dig a well. The fertility of an oasis does not depend on the construction of canals, roads or houses, but on that well. If water springs up everything will have life, if not *nihil*.

The fact is that Jesus told us, 'Without me, nihil.' It is this that I saw in Europe. A crazy army of Catholics is building away at houses, colleges, associations and parties and almost nobody is bothering to dig wells. The result: sadness, discouragement, internal emptiness and sometimes desperation. They are trying to build for God without God.

And don't tell me, sister, that they are praying. No, they're not praying, even if they say a hundred rosaries a day, even if they go to Mass regularly. *Prayer is something quite different!* Prayer is adoration of God and his will, not a jumble of formulae created for the very purpose of smothering the soul and shutting it into the tentacles of habit and the ready-made. Prayer is breathing, love, freedom, inexhaustible dialogue, and above all it is *thinking about God*. This is what is missing from our old-style Christianity, which when it wants to pray starts trotting out formulae. Look at priests. If they prayed seriously, when they came to talk to us they would tell us new things about that God *who is always new* and instead they tell us the same old things and we go out from their preaching without any fervour.

Real prayer – and we have to be mature to understand this – is the silent adoration of God. You put yourself in front of the Blessed Sacrament which is here on Earth just to teach us to pray, and starting from Him – the bridge between the human and the divine – you reach the Father in the thrust of the Spirit. One hour a day, at least, of this sunshine cure gets into the swing of that real prayer which is the starting-point for Heaven. Once our faith becomes lively and strong, then our *being Christian* takes on new flavour and is not just heated-up soup.

I am convinced that if Catholic Action, the militant Congregations and the priests, in short the backbone of the Church, gave *half* its energies to prayer, it would achieve much better results. This is why I left Rome; now I've told you plainly: I too was one of those crazy people, working furiously and not praying sufficiently.

Now I have understood and I want to aim straight at the heart of God: the rest no longer matters to me, or at least it matters only if it enters into God's plan. There are lots of other things to be said, and we will say them, because God willing, this will not be my last letter.

In your letter from Lanzo you are worried again
about my health. I don't understand why. I'm not
fooling you, Dolcidia, I'm *just fine* and this physically
hard life has toughened and rejuvenated me. If in
that letter home I wrote that sentence, it was because
at the time I had a few problems acclimatizing, problems which completely disappeared afterwards.

I have written to Piero[2] to invite him. I really would
like him to come because *afterwards* we could make
the journey to Europe together. You insist as well: I
think it would be an important time.

I'm happy with the summer arrangements for our
old folks. Help them to disentangle the confusion
of their thoughts, especially concerning the future.
Mamma will be naturally inclined to Turin. I will
agree to any solution. Certainly Turin is more their
scene. Perhaps Papà likes Rome better. I don't yet
know Lili's preferences. We shall see.

Give Mother Angela my best wishes and tell her I
send her all the flowers of the Sahara.

To you I send a kiss,

Carlo

10

November 25th '55

My dearest sweetest Dolce,

They have sent on from Beni-Abbès the beautiful
letter which you were so kind to send. You are an
unbeatable secretary and sister! Thank you, thank

you from the depth of my heart, and let me tell you
that you really are my *comfort* and *my joy*.

I am writing to you with a month to go to my
profession, *which with the grace of God I hope to make
at the hands of Piero*. This is all very good, because it
has the air of God's mercy about it and because it fits
in with the sweet plans of the Father's love. It's a pity
you won't be with me (I mean in the body because in
spirit you will definitely be the closest).

On that day – Christmas Day 1955[1] – old Professor
Carretto will be buried beneath the dunes of the
Sahara and it will be left to the jackals in the night
to sing their mournful dirge over his past of compromises and idolatries.

Out of some of his remains will be put together
the new Little Brother 'Charles of Jesus' and with
this name he will go off into the world like a revised
and corrected edition.

Joking apart, my sister, what has happened during
the last year and what, so you tell me, has cost you
a lot of tears, *has been the greatest gift God could give
me*. Perhaps it's due to your prayers for me! For my
part, if there has been any merit it has been due
solely to my simplicity, which at crucial moments in
my life has led me to take decisions which would
have cost others years to mull over. It isn't a virtue,
let's be clear, because it is something inherited from
our parents.

During the year gone by Jesus has come to me
once more.

In a flash I saw the altogether slick and shaky
basis of my so-called apostolate and consequently my
altogether rather false vision of my relationship with

Him. There are moments which if you don't grasp them on the wing are gone for ever.

My mistake was very plain under the headlamps of divine truth.

Do you think, Carlo, that history revolves around people; do you believe in newspapers, politics and the power of words and means; do you believe in yourself, in your potential for good too, in the effectiveness of your activities and your thoughts? All wrong, Carlo my boy. History revolves around me, Christ. I am the *saviour*, not you. I am *the life*.

Think of past civilizations, of the generations gone by: that is what people are worth, that is what people are.

To sum up, my sister, to be consistent with what the light of the Lord gave me in that flash – *experientially*, not through concepts or ideas, there was just one thing to be done: to give up activities, *my* activities and believe in contemplation, that is believe that our duty is *setting ourselves to listen humbly to Jesus* as Mary did, with no other concern, to have no other dream than loving Jesus freely with such a love that it becomes activity, apostolate, salvation.

Dolcidia, take account of the being of God. There are two masters who want you to serve them. The first one gets worked up, acts and builds, and in odd moments comes and tells you how much he has done, and asks you to help him with *his* plans. The other is in love with you and does nothing but love you and gaze at you, and the same thirst for the salvation of the brethren leads Him to a love, from which one can never be separated. Which of the two has more truth about him? The calculation is very simple and is just a question of being consistent.

May God give me the grace of being consistent.

The rest is so much smoke, indeed acrid smoke. To be forgotten, to live a hidden life and to be poor and humble – isn't that the ideal of Christian ascetical life?

How the world ensnares us, sister, even with *L'Osservatore Romano* and *Il Popolo*. We end up stupid and empty, and in that state Satan makes his conquests and reaps his adulation. Die, Dolcidia, die to the world and to yourself and live only in Christ Jesus.

Die to human fuss and be born again in peace, the sweet and incomparable peace which God brought to Earth at the Incarnation; that peace which is not *absence* or *emptiness* but a delicious fullness which floods through our whole personality.

And whose fullness are we dealing with? Nothing less than the presence in us of the Father, the Son and the Holy Spirit. That miracle of love, that dizzy dream of real greatness!

By accepting identification with Christ, the means of our divinization and the pledge of our hope, we enter with Him into the bosom of the Father and begin to live life as His *children*. The Father's grand design is to call us into His family, to make us live life as His children. *This is eternal life, our destiny, our worth*, not what gets stirred up in the world and ends up with its own noisy sound.

Then there are other things which I have tried to get a grip on by accepting the call.

There is *poverty*, which nowadays is not just a religious virtue but has become a sign of contradiction in the world.

The Gospel can no longer be preached by the rich, it goes against the dignity of the apostolate. People no longer believe them. Poverty has been betrayed too often and the pariahs have turned against it.

How will it be possible, sister, to preach in a Communist country in the future unless we get down to the bottom of the social ladder and give a genuine, clear, simple witness to poverty?

The religious life has become too complicated and very often it is no longer seen in its genuine and original brilliance. As a result there are betrayals and misunderstandings concerning the Church and its Authority when it hands on the gospel message. We have to get back to the Gospel and live it out without too much fine print in the contract. Jesus told us that if we believe in His words *we are building our house on rock*. There you are: too many spiritual houses are built on sand because people believe yet don't believe, accept yet don't accept; they're full of compromises.

I know what it is to compromise with the Gospel: unfortunately, I've done it, in part consciously and in part unconsciously. Now I ask the Lord for the grace to be decisive and go all the way. You will help me, won't you? I'm waiting for Piero to let me know the date of his arrival here. Then we will make a ten-day retreat together in the desert. Profession at Christmas and then . . . on our way to Italy.

We will keep you informed of every detail, and if we make the journey by way of Marseilles, we will visit you before Rome.

I'm pleased about Mamma's health. The Lord wants to make us one more gift of a *full* meeting of the family. After that . . . it's what He wants.

I look forward to an intensification of your prayers

for *the success of the retreat, the journey and the general get-together*.

May God bless you with all of His great love for you. I send you a hug and . . . I was about to write a hug for Mother Angela. Just imagine it!

Love, Carlo

11

Rome, January 25th 1956

Dear Dolce,

I have spent a *sweet* two weeks in hospital.

I have the impression that all I have to do now is take a little convalescence to get the strength back into my wheels. I'm very calm and happy: the peace I am enjoying is truly great. It has been – I feel – the gift of my profession.

I have no *regrets* of any kind: I'm on a good road and I want to take it to the end, with the grace of God. I will stay here at least three weeks. I will leave only when I'm completely healed.

Then I will come to Turin and leave from there for France. So we still have the joy of seeing not a little of each other. I repeat my advice to read the Works of St Teresa on contemplative prayer. After that you need to tackle St John of the Cross . . . then that's it because higher than that one cannot go. Only death is higher.

See you soon. I send you a big hug. Carlo

12

Berre,[1] April 22nd 1956

Dearest,

It was right and traditional that this time too my first letter should be from Dolce, my good sister, whose humanness brings tears to the eyes as she struggles continually with the spirit . . . Heartfelt thanks to you and to my dearest Mother Angela, who refines your humanness by her example of balance and wisdom.

Yesterday I spent my first day hidden away in the peace of a work brotherhood. Today, Sunday, I'm on my own because my brethren have gone off to the baptism of one of their workmates.

I spent the whole morning in adoration and now I am getting down to my most urgent correspondence.

To tell you that I'm happy is putting it mildly because I feel myself in the arms of my God.

The life of Nazareth is an immense mystery which eludes human logic. I am well able to bury myself in nothingness and total concealment if the Son of God, *without whom everything is death and without meaning*, was willing to disappear for 30 years into a worker's abject home!

Now I'm here, alone with Him, in a hostile country where nobody knows me and where they watch me doing the shopping with pity because I limp and I'm dressed like a beggar.

Can't you feel, Dolcidia, the beauty of all this?

No triumph is up to this triumph because it is a perfect imitation of Jesus and Mary.

As a town, Berre is to Marseilles what Moncalieri

is to Turin, but more shapeless, sadder and more cosmopolitan. Arab, Greek, Spanish and Italian workers live out their *sad lives* because they are without faith and religious practice. It is a crowd of people who reflect the godless crowds who can be won back only by prayer and sacrifice. And I want to make my life into one single prayer: that is why I left Catholic Action. Help me with your suffering, Dolce, and keep on loving me.

Love, Carlo

13

Berre, June 26th 1956

Dearest Dolce,

Once again I have been silent for too long, but I trust in your indulgence.

I've written instead to Papà for his name day and have replied to a lot of friends who do rather keep on at me.

It's strange how they all want news, and stranger still – at least to me – how elementary knowledge of the contemplative life has been lost in our contemporary Christian community. They all find my present life strange, whereas in reality it's the simplest thing in the world. Why should a life of poverty be surprising when it is part and parcel of every religious profession, when it is the simplest call of Jesus in the Gospel? But what stuns our so-called Christians most is seeing a rejection of the organized, dynamic, 'high-profile' apostolate.

But did not Jesus put it plainly to Martha? And isn't the whole tradition of the Church a witness to the primacy of prayer over action? Isn't this what Our Lady did? Isn't this what the Little Flower did?

It takes patience, my dear Dolce, and pushing ahead with great fidelity.

I have received a long letter from Pietro, but still nothing from Lili. Our youngest sister is a real masterpiece of epistolary laziness!

Hand this sheet on to Emerenziana, who has also got good reason to complain about me. This summer I advise you to re-read the Little Flower's *History of a Soul*. It's still the masterpiece of modern sainthood. I like her poems too. Lots of kisses.

Love, Carlo

Warm and friendly greetings to Mother Angela.

14

Berre, June 29th 1956

Dearest Dolce,

Our letters have crossed and I'm returning to the subject again particularly because of your concern regarding [. . .].

I can very well understand our friend's silence: recently the town council for the municipality of Turin had to be set up and he is nothing less than no. 2, immediately below the mayor. His muteness is very understandable given that he had so much else on his mind.

As regards the accommodation question, don't bother yourself at all; let it stand and don't make any more requests: after all he is the alderman in charge of Finance and therefore specifically in charge of the appropriate procedure. It's up to him to answer you, but don't you worry him about time. I know well, very well, the way politicians operate, and therefore I understand their slowness over certain procedures.

But be calm: he is really a good friend and will sort the matter out. When you see him or telephone him give him my congratulations on his victory and tell him I'm praying for him.

Speaking of prayer reminds me of your spiritual exercises, for which I have prayed a lot, and from which I hope you have emerged with plans for *childhood* and *love*.

Once, when we were younger, I told you to concentrate on the will. Now I tell you: concentrate on your littleness. Make yourself little, little, consider yourself 'nothing', don't make spiritual plans but abandon yourself totally to the action of God. All our plans, even on the road to holiness, are perfectly useless: the real plan is in His hand and we need to go to Him like children seeking love.

That's all there is to it: even the Eucharist will pass away, and only love with remain because it is our final perfection. God is love and we will be immersed in Him in proportion to the love we have shown in life. Because the Cross is just a higher degree of love, our consummation. May God bless you.

Lots of kisses, Carlo

15

Marseilles, July 16th 1956

Dear Dolce,

A couple of lines from this city, where we have spent a lovely day, just to tell you that I have been transferred (at least for this summer) from Berre to St Remy.

Fr Voillaume needed me for some editorial work and called for me urgently. In fact I'm passing through here and I'm taking the train this evening for Dijon.

Here is my address for you:

Fraternité St Remy[1]
   near Montbard (Côte d'Or).

Everything is going smoothly and I'm very happy.

The spirit of Jesus and the Father is embedding itself in my heart and I am experiencing more and more what love is. I want to become little so that I can run more swiftly towards the great final fire. Go on, my sister, no holding back, just trust in the immense mercy of One who immolated His Son to save a slave.

Love, Carlo

16

St Remy, July 31st 1956

Dearest: Bishop Piero, Sr Emerenziana, Sr Dolcidia and Liliana, that is my dearest Brother and Sisters.

This time I want to write you a collective letter because the things which fill my heart and which I would tell you are the same and because, being as poor in terms of time as in terms of everything else, I'll make a saving.

It won't become a habit, however, because it wouldn't be good, given that nothing is more personal than correspondence. I say this for Dolce [Sweet], who being fond of correspondence would not put up with it at all and would be quick to call me to order . . . sweetly.

To begin with, some news of what has been going on. As you will already know, I have left Berre for a time. Father Voillaume, needing me for some editorial work, requested me to help him and has summoned me here to the peace of St Remy, perhaps for two months. I wasn't put out by it, both because obedience is always sweet and sure, and because St Remy is an adoration Brotherhood where, as at El Abiodh, there is more commitment and calm about prayer. Therefore I will spend my holidays here and finish, I hope, with a fortnight's retreat at St Gildas[1] – a little island off Brittany, where we also have an adoration Brotherhood. St Remy is a village on the outskirts of Dijon; the countryside is beginning to have a northern look about it and has all the characteristics of bygone France.

Now that I've got to tell you about myself and my affairs, I would call this chapter, 'De felicitate plena.'

Already 7 months have passed since I left my African Novitiate to begin a rougher experience than the one I had at El Abiodh, but even so it seems to me to be just the dawn of real joy. The Lord is giving Himself to me with such fullness that I remain wounded in the very depth of my being. El Abiodh was the physical desert; a desert which prepared me for the stripping of the mind: a work Brotherhood strips you hour by hour and leads you to the nakedness of the Cross. The desert had its human fascination, its mysterious appeal even on an artistic and cultural level; Berre, with its dirt and its bedbugs, takes away even that fascination and leads you, a beggar among beggars. To have no hope except Heaven, no joy except love and prayer.

I've written to a friend who feels I've got my back to the wall and no means of escape. And it's true.

In a lukewarm moment, some people can fall back on books, others on girlfriends or boyfriends, others again on activity, but we have nothing to fall back on except Chapel. Everything outside that is ugly, because on a human level poverty is altogether ugly, and we are surrounded by poverty because we are poor.

I remember that in Catholic Action I could find distraction in meetings, conferences, action. I even had a taste for talking about God even though I was far from Him and afraid to spend one hour *alone* with Him. Now I can't do that any more. I don't have activities, I don't have meetings, I don't have conferences, I don't have anything. It's the stripping away of everything.

Living in a tiny house like the Brotherhood's, with Jesus listening to your breathing while you sleep, listening to the noise of your eating so thin are the walls, causes you either to live totally on faith and therefore to feel yourself at home with Him as at Nazareth or to live in sadness or worse desperation. A big house with courtyards, corridors and bedrooms can give you the feeling that you can hide a bit from Him, but a little shack doesn't give you this feeling. And so, either you live on faith, and all is joy, because you feel face to face with Him, or . . . you run away.

I've tried to paint you a vivid picture of the house in order to tell you something very important, which is perhaps the deepest treasure I am uncovering among the 'Petits Frères'; the stripping away, *the beatitude of poverty*. I had never enjoyed it so much in my life.

I used to think that poverty was just a shortage of means, but it is something quite different. The shortage of means, living just for the day with trust in the Father, and not worrying any more about clothing, is just the gateway to the immense temple of poverty.

Real poverty is feeling yourself to be *nothing* because you possess *nothing*.

It is a poverty in spirit which has no more pretensions, which no longer relies on itself because it has nothing, which counts for nothing. I would say that it is the *shape of humility*, *the outward garment of humility*.

I have always trusted in the Father's providence, and I have always experienced poverty as detachment from the goods of Earth. But . . . what pride I had in my internal treasures, my ideas, my schemes! They were my riches. *I was rich*. I felt myself to be so rich that I could even give to the Church, give to my brethren, save them, save them.

What a wretch I was! This was sin! What could I give my brethren? Words, empty words!

I could do nothing because I am nothing, I have nothing. There is only one Giver: the Father; there is only one Redeemer: Jesus; there is only one Sanctifier: the Holy Spirit. To plunge into this reality, to discover these truths, that is the real stripping, that is becoming like little children, taking pleasure in one's own nothingness, loving simple, real and genuine things; and getting away from rhetoric.

And it is in the course of this stripping that God gives himself to us, and it is in the midst of this annihilation that Jesus grows in us.

I seem to have taken on a new life; I see the world in a new light.

Once the 'I' has been taken away, once the worries about oneself, one's own glory and one's own future have been dissolved, the soul is relieved of immense weights which crushed it, tortured it and bore down upon it. It feels light and free, it seems to be flying.

There then begins the real Christian experience which can be summed up in one word: *loving*.

The void created by the stripping away of self *is filled with God who is Love*. It is the encounter with the Bridegroom, it is the blessedness of union.

'Oh, set me like a seal on your heart, like a seal on your arm. For love is strong as Death, jealousy relentless as Sheol. The flash of it is a flash of fire, a flame of Yahweh himself. Love no flood can quench, no torrents drown.'

The encounter with one's brethren is also in God because love of them is the same as the first kind of love.

Loving our brethren in their reality, in their poverty, in their littleness; that's all there is to it: anything else is trickery and a waste of time.

What a magnificent programme, my dear Brother and Sisters! Oh, help me to live it out, pray that

I may come to the threshold of contemplation and love!

Nothing else matters to me any more: it's dead matter to me.

I have experienced the glory and the fullness of realizing the personality: what bitter things!

We are never so far from the truth as when we feel great and full of ourselves.

The truth is that there is only God, that it is He who guides the world, that it is He who saves.

What a fatal error many Christians live in when they think of themselves as saviours, when they get worked up as if everything depended on them. How deeply I have fallen into this error!

Now I'm beginning to feel by experience what it is to be nothing, to be capable of nothing, to know nothing, and this is why my gaze is fixed with more concern and joy on God, breathing in life and truth from Him and becoming blessedly full of His presence and His reality.

Oh the sweet hours of adoration I have passed, no longer in contemplation of myself but of Him, only Him; no longer even passed in supplication but only in the enjoyment of His presence, His love and His greatness!

Oh the divine littleness to which Jesus invites us: 'Become like this child', which allows us to contemplate the Father, the giver of life and happiness!

I really don't know how I have been able to have from God such a great grace to end my life in a school that is so pure and sweet.

It's the desert in which these people lived for 20 years which has allowed them to come up with a deeper spirituality, getting it under way again after too many rhetorical complications. What it comes down to is nothing less than a return to the Gospel with greater faith and more simplicity. Therefore, I was quite right to call this chapter 'De felicitate pleena'.

I'm happy even though I've got to kill bed bugs and live in a hovel without toilets.

Write to me here at St Remy; then I'll keep you up to date.

Dolce, I would ask you to assure my revered Mother Angela of my poor but constant prayer, and pass my regards on to her.

Affectionate kisses to you, Bishop Piero, Sr Emerenziana and Lili, with an invitation to walk as closely roped together as mountain climbers, helping one another on towards the heavenly Jerusalem.

Your little Carlo

17

St Gildas, September 18th 1956

My Dearest Bishop Peter, Sr Emerenziana, Sr Dolce and Liliana,

Yet again, excuse me, I'm having recourse to the system of a collective letter because I'm behind in my correspondence with all of you and because I've just come through a really exceptional period of my life.

As you can see, I'm writing to you again from St Gildas, where I'm finishing my long retreat. This year Father Voillaume, who is my Superior, gave me a lovely gift. In practical terms, he had me spend the summer in two adoration Brotherhoods, or, as we prefer to say, 'desert' Brotherhoods.

First, on the grounds of compiling the Syriac liturgy (which I did) he had me spend more than a month at St Remy on the Côte d'Or near Dijon; then, thinking to prepare me for the missionary exhibition in Nantes, he sent me here to St Gildas.

St Gildas is a tiny little island off Brittany (we Little Brothers are alone on the island and – precisely because of the solitude – we call it a desert Brotherhood).

At the moment of writing to you (it's almost 9:00 pm.) I'm in a little hermitage on the island. It's a cave of the kind . . . at El Abiodh but slightly better furnished: there's a candle, a little window and a little camp bed.

We are building several similar hermitages among the rocks on the island to allow the Brothers who come here to get away for prayer and adoration.

For me it has been a 'godsend' and in practice I have spent more than a month in real retreat.

According to Father's plan, I could have stayed here right up to October 16th (the opening day of the Exhibition in Nantes) but . . . my friends in Berre kicked up a storm to have me return and so . . . goodbye Nantes, goodbye St Gildas.

As you can see, my fortunes are rising by the day, and I cannot do less than tell you about some conclusions reached in this genuine desert period.

First, however, I'd like to reply to a sentence of Dolce's about my work. She wrote to me at St Remy: 'I'm happy with your new editorial work which of course I consider more appropriate etc. etc.' I have got to say that my sister – and she is not just a religious but a Salesian, and therefore a disciple of a Saint who knew all about manual labour and understood it inside out – *still hasn't understood a thing* and makes a distinction between one kind of work and another, and setting up intellectual work as having priority over such-and-such work. She still hasn't *tasted* the sweet reality that there is no difference between a cobbler and the Minister for Education; between a Sister who peels potatoes and another who teaches philosophy. Or at least, if a scale is to be drawn up and a pecking order is to be established, it should be done by looking at who shares most closely in the suffering of the Cross and the imitation of our sweet Master, Jesus, in His humility, His truth, His concealment and, I would go on to say, in His *abjection*.

Because this is the law of the Christian, quite different from the law of the world, which is primacy, supremacy, intelligence, dominion, power, riches. But it is difficult to understand this – or rather to live it – and . . . certain highly-placed Sisters, accustomed to moving in high circles, attending receptions and, in a word, the exercise of power, end up by thinking that their brother would be better off as a lecturer or a minister instead of being a dishwasher or a manual labourer.

I've been teasing my poor, dear, saintly Dolcidia, who has a thousand times more goodness than me, who is a thousand times more accustomed to discipline and the Cross than her 'Little Brother' brother, only to bring home a concept which from now on has to be held in common if we are to understand each other and walk together benefitting from each other's experience.

Now we come to my deeper insights during this sweet period of prayer. I would give them this title, making use of a quotation from John: '*I will reveal myself to you.*' This is Jesus speaking at the Last Supper, promising a revelation of Himself to those who do His will. You see, up to now I have experienced God's revelation mostly through Nature (I've always liked it a lot), through history (my dear St Augustine), or through social events (the struggle in defence of the poor as human beings), or through the study of theology (how much meditation I've done, how many books I've read!). For some little time however – and this coincides with my joining a contemplative Order – I've experienced more of another sort of revelation, the intimate, personal one of Jesus. I couldn't tell you a lot about it if you asked me for details, but I would tell you one thing: 'I feel I know Him as a Person rather than as a Trinity.' I can say about Him: 'I know Him.'

I no longer need to watch a sunset to think about God; I don't even need to read books of meditations: it's enough for me to stay silent before Jesus in the Blessed Sacrament. It's He who talks to me. Oh how true is the sentence, 'I will reveal myself to you!'

And this is real revelation, the principle of eternal life: 'this is eternal life: that they should know You, Father, and Him whom you have sent, Jesus.' It is He who speaks and you have to stand alone in the nakedness of faith before Him. No more formulae, no more problems, no more intellectual worries. The soul opens itself up to the action of the Spirit *in a passivity made up of love and not of thoughts*. What do we know of God? Does the greatest theologian know more about Him than a peasant woman? Not at all.

When it comes to real, wholesome, personal knowledge of God we are all equal: we know nothing about Him. But He, by revealing Himself, makes Himself known *and this knowledge is eternal life*. And this knowledge is possible for everybody, because in this we are all equal. This is why in Christianity an ignorant peasant woman is worth as much as a great scholar. If it were a question of intelligence or wisdom *God would really have created injustices:* but instead it's a question of love and we're all capable of loving in the same way.

God is just, sister Dolce, and the most ignorant Sister can become a saint while the most intellectual Sister can stay wrapped up in herself churning over her useless thoughts. Don't you agree?

And now, to end, I'm telling you that the hardest work I've had to do – grasp the truth of this – has been that of becoming passive before God. Previously 'I did everything' myself; now I try to leave it up to Him.

It is not easy, presumptuous as I am, but I'm trying. To keep quiet and adore: this is the atmosphere in which the revelation of God unfolds. And to believe that we really are nothing, that we can do nothing (how am I going to get it right into my head?) and to leave it up to Him. To stay before Him as though taking a cure in the sun, without thoughts and useless worries. *Just loving, loving, loving*. And love is a truth which if it's there there's no point in saying so: it's just there. Enough for now. See you in Berre. Kisses to all 4 of you . . .

Your Little Brother, Carlo

18

St Gildas, September 19th 1956

Dearest, sweetest Dolce,

I have received your letter of the 15th and it has caused me a *strong pang of remorse* for my long silence. I therefore took up my pen and . . . out came a long epistle which I despatched to you like the Minister for the PP.TT. (as they say in France).

Thanks for the news from home. In fact (I'm talking about my sister Liliana's rare ability to absolve herself from correspondence) she wrote to me from her resting-place in the Abbruzzi. Nothing is settled yet. Still she seems much at peace and to have a real desire to do the Lord's will.

Let us continue to pray.

Next I'll answer your questions, and I apologize for not having done so before. I received both the copy of Curti's letter (if Papà comes to Turin, go to him together, explanations are better done verbally) and the copy of the photo of Papà and Mamma. It was a kind thought and I'm grateful to you for it.

Tell Mother Angela that I continue to pray a lot for her and that I thank her for her kind, very kind greetings. She is a very astute woman in whom religious consecration has sublimated nature without creating problems. This is the miracle of simplicity which is fairly common in Salesian circles!

Have you ever thought about the Virgin in relation to Jesus? Her greatest merit was retaining her simplicity despite the fact that she knew Him to be the Son of God, to the point that she could even rebuke Him! Tell the truth: would you have got down on your knees to talk to Him? You see, it's because you're not yet simple!!! I'm joking!

Lots of kisses just for you, Carlo

19

Berre, December 7th 1956

Dear, dearest Dolce,

I can imagine your expectation, especially after your kind gesture in sending 300 francs . . . followed by an appeal to divine Providence! What would you have me say? The trouble with life in the Brotherhood is that the doors have no locks, which means they can't be kept shut, which means you can't get five minutes' peace to write to your sister the way you'd like to.

I should go and write in the chapel – the only calm and quiet place – but I haven't got myself set up for that yet.

Have patience, and above all don't think that I have forgotten you.

So thank you for the francs, which I will turn into stamps and thanks even more for my never-praised-enough Mother Angela who was their . . . happy inspiration. I've no great news about my life except what I'm discovering in prayer, and this comes under just two headings: *we never see sufficiently our nothing-ness, and we are never able to grasp the immense, oceanic, infinite love of God*. Who art Thou and who am I? asked my charming and truly fine Catherine of Siena, and from these two poles she struck the brightest flames of love possible for a woman on this chilly Earth. How difficult it is to be *little*, my sister! How hard it is to feel ourselves to be what we are in reality: nothing, nothing, nothing! And on the anvil of this error we forge all our sadness and let ourselves be blown away by the useless wind of our worries. Be little like Jesus in Bethlehem! Writhe no more but rest quietly in Our Lady's arms, even if Herod's furious slaughter is going on outside. Unfortunately, our error is 'to want to do it our way', 'to feel ourselves to be somebody', 'to trust in our own plans', 'not to give due weight to the Father's plan'. It's frightening, my sister, the extent to which hidden pride burns the soul and dries up everything. And pride is all the greater in spiritual people: in us. I can understand why Jesus took a bitter line when dealing with us (the professionally religious): sinners and prostitutes will take their place ahead of us.

It's because we don't want to be little! On the excuse that the religious life is a great, very great thing, we no longer dream *of becoming nothing, nothing, nothing*.

Dear Dolce, I would ask that if you pray at the crib for your brother Carlo, ask with enthusiasm for this gift for me: make him little, little, little. All right?

All my respects to Mother Angela and a very warm hug to you.

Carlo

20

Berre, January 3rd 1957

Dearest Dolce and dearest Emerenziana,

You are right to complain about me, but if you knew my situation you would give me a full pardon.

One of the *poverties* to which I have to accustom myself is that of not being able to write. It's hard but that's the way it is.

The unlocked doors take all your silence away, the work tires you out, and the long hours of prayer cut down the available time. What's left?

To suffer and to love.

Fortunately you don't lose out because you are always there at my offertory, but I know it can't be pleasant.

I spent a fairly painful Christmas, but as a result I felt more at ease in the nakedness of Bethlehem. It's strange, but true: you cannot understand the poverty of Jesus if you are rich and lack nothing . . .

As a result I feel happier because poorer. Thanks to Dolce for her prayer, 'make him little little'. That's all there is to it: it's the pledge we make in order to enter the Kingdom. *Otherwise there's no getting in and Jesus says so clearly*.

I wish you a year of real *childhood*. Do away with your problems: live without problems: love is the only thing which isn't a problem.

And . . . see you in a month. Lots of kisses.

Your Little Brother, Carlo

21

Rome, February 19th 1957

Dear Dolce,

As I told you on the telephone, radiography[1] has shown up . . . a piece of needle in the nerve. The matter is very important because it shed light on the slowness of the healing.

I think I will have to undergo a little operation.

I am sure of your prayers, that even in these secondary matters the sweet will of God may always be done.

Yours, Carlo

22

Almost in Marseilles[1], March 7th 1957

The journey is going normally.

I'm beginning to get the smell of France. I left everything in peace at home. I am . . . more convinced about my departure, I would say . . . almost happy.

Within the inside of a month I shall leave for Africa. Long live solitude!

Lots of kisses, Carlo

23

Marseilles,[1] March 13th 1957

My dear sister,

By the time you receive this postcard I shall already be in *Algeria*, where I shall stay *for a fortnight*. At the beginning of April I shall leave for my final destination: *Tamanrasset*.[2]

I will write to you from Algeria and I will put my address on the back. I left Berre yesterday with *much sadness* mixed with *much joy* at taking up again my life in the desert, which I consider a great grace for my soul. Write a few words to me in Algeria and then I'll tell you about my new work. There are many bright missionary prospects. But I'll write to you about it.

Lots of kisses to you and warmest greetings to Mother Angela.

Your Little Brother, Carlo

24

Algiers, March 19th 1957

Darling Dolce,

My first letter – sent on to me from Berre – *naturally* had to be yours. I received it today, the feast of St Joseph, which here in Africa, as in France, is not a holiday of obligation.

Thanks for your never-ending solicitude, from which many Carrettos could learn, myself included.

As you can see, here I am again in Africa. It was a rather more rushed departure than I expected. The work at which I will be employed was pressing, and as soon as I reached Marseilles I had to pack my bags again.

I wasn't sorry about it because I already knew that I had to leave Berre and my duties attracted me.

I made the crossing for free on a French cargo ship – the only passenger with 21 sailors – but given the sea and the small size of the boat, *I paid for it* with everything which might have been in my stomach, which was furious at the rude heaving.

In Algiers I am the guest of the little Brotherhood which Piero saw 15 months ago and which is situated on an American *garbage dump* at Hussen-Dey. The Brotherhood has 4 Brothers, each one more magnificent than the next and rich in the only treasure which matters: charity.

I have been in touch with the University of Algiers. You know what it consists of, in outline. Hydrological and meteorological data have to be collected from a large area of desert around Tamanrasset. A powerful military jeep has been handed over to me, in which I shall travel the endless tracks of the desert. This is to earn me my bread, in accordance with the Rule. Moreover, on top of the work, there will be a missionary apostolate, and for this Father has given me a long series of Tuareg villages and oases which I am to visit with another Brother in order to make missionary contact in accordance with that rule of love and friendship which is ours.

There is no point in telling you that I'm happy. Africa, silence, the desert, prayer, stripping away, poverty: these are powerful appeals to my soul, even

if the life on the tracks which awaits me is of a harshness made up of heat, cold, thirst and things of that
kind.

I will have to rely on you this time, sister, because
the timetable foreseen is one in which our tent is our
chapel and the desert our daily resting-place. I will
have to spend a few days a month at the base in
Tamanrasset.

For the time being, I shall stay here in Algiers until
March 31st. On April 1st I will set out for the south
with all the equipment which the University of Algiers has made available to me.

As you can see, everything is going fine. I will
have all the time I need for prayer and all the silence
I need for intimacy with God, and all the charity I
need for the Tuareg, who will be my tribe.

I'll write to you again.

Make a copy of this letter for Piero, to whom I now
feel myself more closely bound in missionary work.
I send you a warm hug while I send equally warm
greetings to Mother Angela.

                                                    Carlo

25

Algiers, March 25th 1957

Dearest Dolce,

Just a couple of lines to tell you how joyful I am
to have received your letter of the 21st . . . Thanks.

You are always my Dolce [Sweet] and you know
how to make me feel deeply consoled.

Today, the feast of the Annunciation, I'm here in the 'tincanville' of Algiers, close to Jesus. It's an American shanty town built out of tin cans and is already feeling the heat of the African sun, even though it's only March.

But Jesus is here and I think his home in Nazareth was neither prettier nor more comfortable.

I'm continuing my course at the University of Algiers and everything is going well.

My departure for the south is fixed for April 1st, and if you look at a map you will see that I have to travel 1,375 miles to reach the Hoggar, the mountains where Charles de Foucauld was killed.

There we have 4 mission stations and a hermitage where we will spend our periods of desert and adoration. I will send you a photo from down there. For the time being I'm sending you a photo of our Brotherhood here. Not bad . . . is it?

Don't worry, sister. There's a madness in the Gospel which has to be lived with . . . when He calls.

And then . . . you know that He is a *jealous God!* This why He wants me to bury myself down there, *alone with Him*.

Could there be a finer adventure?

Dear Dolce, get a Bible, open it at the Song of Songs, go to the chapel and read it all very slowly. You will see that I'm right to go down there. Ciao.

Love, Carlo

26

Algiers,[1] March 31st 1957

The jeep is ready with the tent and supplies.

Tomorrow morning I'm setting out for the Sahara and I shall cross it in a fortnight. Please, be calm. Everything will go well. I count on you to pray a lot.

Kisses, Carlo

27

April 1st 1957[1]

I celebrated the 47th year of my foundation among the palm trees and sand of the Sahara. This evening I reached the 393rd mile. Now I'm going to sleep because I'm tired.

Good night, sister,

Carlo

28

Assekrem,[1] July 5th 1957

My Dearest Dolce,

I'm writing to you from the hermitage at Assekrem, which is the very one built by Charles de Foucauld. It's a little stone and mud building situated on a plateau 2,925 metres up. It might be said that the plateau dominates the whole of the Hoggar massif

and Charles de Foucauld must have chosen it both
for its wild and savage beauty, supremely suited to
prayer, and to be able to help the Tuareg, who during
the summer come with their camels and goats in
search of a bit of pasture.

I've done no work today because I want to devote
myself completely to prayer and correspondence.
The Brother who was with me yesterday evening was
called out to a sick person last night and left at 11:00
pm. He will certainly have travelled all night because
the sick person is 50 miles from here. He will not be
back until tomorrow or the day after.

Meanwhile I'm alone and that's a great thing for
somebody who wants to pray!

I want to reply to your last letter of June 13th,
which reached me only a few days ago when I passed
through Tam (as regards correspondence, just write
on ordinary paper with ordinary postage. Post for
Algeria goes first to France and from France is sent
here by aeroplane. All of it. Therefore airmail letters
are useless). You raise two problems and I would
like to reply to them so as to leave you as calm as
possible.

1) *The question of the telephone caller:* either she's
hysterically sick or she can't hear on the telephone.
Take your pick. When she spoke to me about a fake
marriage for an invalid friend, I told her that it was
necessary rather to make a real marriage when the
opportunity arose. And the opportunity was an old
and lonely man in search of a human being whom
he could help spiritually and materially for the whole
of her life. A real marriage, in fact, between two
people who wanted to support one another even if,
for reasons of health and age, the marriage would

certainly not have been consummated and therefore without children.

I went on to tell the young lady that in order to have this opportunity she must pray and wait. For my part, I would do my best to take advantage if the desired opportunity should *arise* among my acquaintances.

But I never spoke of a sure thing, already fixed up, etc., etc. Therefore I think the young lady has just been dreaming or is altogether rather excitable [. . .].

2) The other thing you speak of is *the problem of the house*. I must admit, my dear sister, that sometimes I'm disgusted by certain reactions in our house concerning *my affairs*. When it comes down to it, I'm the one who should be troubled about the loss of money (if there should be a loss). The money is mine. What has it got to do with other people? Are they going short?

At home there's Papà's pension, mine, and the rent on the house in Turin. There is no shortage of bread in a house with these secure incomes and I'm deeply pained to hear remarks from such unchristian quarters which are so out of tune with abandonment into the hands of Providence.

If it's possible to get back the amount lent even in part – as I hope will be a bonus – we shall give thanks to the Lord, but to suffer like Papà is doing is really useless. To talk about collapses . . . is altogether pagan. To go on to criticize the folly of having lent the money is offensive. It is not the first time that there has been a failure in business and it's not even something to be amazed about. It's a risk. It could have been put in the bank, true, but at half the interest rate. In any case, one's own money is for paying out personally, and in my life I have always tried to pay personally. I haven't regretted it even if sometimes I've taken a risk.

You tell me, 'Lili's marriage might depend on those few pence.' I don't believe it. Firstly because what I promised Lili for her dowry will come out of my war damages. Secondly, Mario – and this is to his credit – became engaged to Lili precisely at the awkward moment. This suggests that he is a fine man who is not marrying Lili for her money. This is perhaps what I like best about the affair. Mario did not wait until the matter was resolved before getting engaged but did so in the thick of things; this is very good and says a lot about him.

I really would like you, my sister, to keep in closer contact and help those at home to stay calm and relaxed. At such a splendid time as that of Lili's engagement, instead of thanking the Lord for the great gift received, there is moaning and talking of collapses . . . It is Goodbye to common sense, not to say 'goodbye to a living faith'.

All right?

The news about Piero's probable arrival for the Congress is good. It would be a good occasion for the marriage. I'll try to come too, if the Lord so wishes. I'm not talking about you two – yourself and Emerenziana - . . . I understand, but we brothers have certain duties . . . to protect Lili. She's the youngest!

I'll leave you now because adoration is waiting for me. Praying up here is so beautiful. Last night I got up and spent a little time alone with Jesus.

What a gift the Lord gave me, sister, by calling me to consecrate my life to prayer alone!

I've done a fair amount of work, haven't I? I've kept busy, haven't I? I've walked, run, flown and met thousands upon thousands of people. Now I'm shut up with Him alone. In the garden of love. As for souls, I talk to Him about them and their salvation. It doesn't seem a waste of time to me, and after all . . . it's what He wanted, He's the one who called me, therefore I'm happy. Little sister, I send you a big hug in Him.

Love, Carlo

29

Assekrem, August 2nd 1957

Dearest Sweet Dolce,

I'm writing to you from the hermitage at Assekrem where I'm staying. On my way through Tam I picked up your precious letter, or rather two of them, and I'm grateful for the dear and lovely things you tell me. I'm pleased you've regained your peace over our loved ones. Remember, Dolce, that God is watching over them. I would say . . . *He is involved by our very absence*. What we can no longer do, called as we are to other duties, *He* is taking care of . . . and better than we who cannot do much: keep calm. As for the telephone caller, I really have the feeling that she is a bit carried away; calm her down patiently, above all with the thought that life would be altogether too convenient if she could get a perpetual 'free' annuity. Don't you think so?

It's a long time since I had anything from Lili but I'm used to that and I'm not worried. I pray a lot for her and that's enough for me. I feel that the Lord is guiding her and I'm happy. Once she's settled, all that's left is for us to live out to the full our vocation without hesitations or external worries. There's still a long way to go.

My life continues for the better and I feel more and more that the Lord wanted me here. I have a lot of responsibility if I am to be equal to the gift, but I have a very great deal of confidence in Our Lady's help. I feel she is particularly close to me and she is my mistress in prayer.

The leg is slowly getting better and I can already take long walks for my work. I'm waiting to hear from Piero: I do hope that he will come for the World Congress on the Apostolate. That would make a good date for Lili's wedding.

Ciao, sister, pass my news on to Emerenziana.

Love,

Carlo

30

Tam, October 19th 1957

Dear Dolce,

Passing through Tam I've come across your lovely, long dear letter. Among other things I see you are concerned about writings from your old brother (Carlo).

I'll write to you at length next week when I spend two days' rest at Assekrem.

Now I've got to set off again immediately.

I'll send you a photo which you'll like.

Ciao,

Carlo

P.S. I'm also in debt to the great and good Mother Angela. Tell her that she's in my heart and prayers every day.

Ciao, I'll write to her soon.

31

Tam, Christmas 1957

Dear sister Dolce,

I'm sure that you're worried by my silence towards you, but this time I don't even ask your pardon. I would like you once and for all to learn to understand me. I'm not able to write at the dictates of social convention, and sometimes not even at those of affection. I've got to wait for the right moment, the moment in which a letter means something, above all 'rings true', and it's not easy, my sweet sister. You'll have to excuse me, but that's the way I'm made, and you mustn't worry yourself. You're better at it than I am and use a different method, on the goodness of which everybody is agreed, *including the undersigned!* It will be difficult for me to change unless in Purgatory. But we'll have to see how the post works there.

Thanks then for your last letter and the good news. I'm happy that Piero will be present at the wedding. I shall not come and I want to make this sacrifice for the family-to-be. I haven't even put in a request to Father Prior, which he would have granted. I feel that it should be so, that I should not go and that – for everybody's good – I should stay in Africa. A friend has paid my fare. I have taken the money and sent it to Lili for her honeymoon. It will come in useful and I shall spend the whole day praying in some obscure corner of the desert. Don't be angry, after all you know I'm stubborn and don't change. In any case, the presence of Piero, a Bishop, will fill the house and the couple will be happy.

Afterwards I have invited Piero to come here. After his stay in Italy, 10 days' retreat here would do him good. Who can tell? I don't even dare to hope for it, but Providence is so generous: God is so much a God of the impossible that . . . we shall see.

I hope that you spent a good Christmas. I've prayed a lot for you. I have asked Our Lady that she might give you a spirit 'de petitesse'; I have asked Jesus that He might make you understand more and more the value of poverty, which is an understanding of our wretchedness, our nothingness, our being like Jesus in Bethlehem, twigs at the mercy of history, defenceless, powerless and without money in the hands of arrogant masters.

The Christ child is the real model of this 'littleness', this poverty, this nothingness.

And yet He was All.

God lacked nothing, but there was just one thing

He did not have, did not know about: littleness, weakness. He wanted to experience it in Jesus and there, right there, He showed us the right relationship between creature and Creator.

Now have you prayed for me? I'm sure of it, because I feel your love and it does me good.

Why do you always tell me to 'pray for Emerenziana and her Community'?

One last thing. Try to get me another map of the skies like the last one, from Paravia. Gazing at the stars is always a part of my night's rest and here in the South there are some constellations which I don't yet know.

Ciao dear sister, happy 1958 (I'm waiting for a little calendar).

Give my regards to all the Rev. Sisters you meet who know me.

Have a Christmas hug from your brother

Carlo

32

Assekrem, February 18th 1958

My ever dearest sister,

As you can see I'm back in the hermitage at Assekrem. I wanted to begin this Lent of 1958 here and Providence has let me do so. A few days ago I climbed up here and I shall stay here for ten days or so. I'm alone, alone, completely alone, 50 miles from Tam and 3,250 feet up in this little hermitage, with the sole aim of being day and night in the company of Jesus, my only companion in the hermitage. As you can see, I could not be happier. I celebrated today – Shrove Tuesday – with a large post bag which reached me via a tourist passing through. I say 'celebrated' because there was . . . finally a letter from Lili in Grosseto and the splendid news that a former colleague[1] of mine in the apostolate is to enter about now the Mount Sion Carmel in the Holy Land.

From Lili I had news about you (never in short supply, thanks to God and your good will) and about Piero, who had the kindness to write to me as he was about to leave Rome. The wedding has been a beautiful gift.

I can assure you, Dolcidia, that I felt freed from a burden. It was a responsibility of mine, particularly since I left Lili alone unexpectedly. Never in my life have I prayed for someone as I did for Lili on this occasion. I felt that the Lord would help us by fixing up our youngest little sister. At any rate I stormed Heaven with all my well-known arrogance. Mario is a good lad, a cheerful, diligent Christian. I could not hope for a better for Lili.

And may Heaven be thanked!

They will not lack trials; they have four old folks on their shoulders, and not an easy situation: all things designed on purpose to make a marriage virtuous. I can assure you that I saw the hand of God especially in the financial adversities.

It would have been too easy and too pagan to start a family, a love and a life in common 'all fixed up'. God has the knowledge, God has the power, and I believe the liquidation of the . . . little nest-egg will have been an act of love. In future they will be able to say, 'We have paid, we have suffered.' And you know, sister, the irreplaceable function of pain and trials in life.

So don't be afraid but soldier on with more faith and more love.

Changing the subject, I have to thank you for the parcel which reached me a few days ago. Heartfelt thanks for the map of the skies and . . . your letters.

As regards the heavens – or at least the astronomical ones – I'm now quite an expert. Almost every night I get up to study the stars and I know them by name, colour and size. I use a little pair of binoculars, especially here at Assekrem, and it has become my favourite diversion. The notepaper will certainly come in useful. Which reminds me, you mustn't worry if sometimes I don't write. I'll be more conscientious in future, but don't bank on it. Ask your guardian angel to speak nicely to my guardian angel. That way, when he nudges me I shall know how to write you nice letters the way you like them.

How I would like to tell you so many things, Dolcidia! To tell you what I feel inside. But it's so difficult! The moment certain interior things are hinted at, they become spoiled. It's so difficult to be *true*, *simple* and *humble* in correspondence.

And then I have especial difficulty discerning within and I almost always end up (the pencil's given out) by being unhappy with what I've written. What's more, I admit that I have a certain fear about writing to you. I know you take everything I write seriously and I have to be especially careful.

This is the reason why – as I was saying – I don't always manage to write to you, even though I want to.

Do you understand?

Now I'll look for another pencil stub.

Here we are: I've found one.

So I was telling you that you're the kind of person who takes everything seriously. And it's true. Above all the spiritual life. Sometimes you give me the feeling that you want to climb the highest mountains on your hands and knees. It's love which drives you on, and I'm certain that the Holy Spirit will lead you high, very high.

And He will lead you higher still if you put into operation a system which I have discovered only recently: 'Walk standing still.' That is, be terribly active and at the same time totally passive. Incline your will, but keep very still before God. Don't move. Don't even move your lips, listen in silence. It's up to Him to speak, it's up to Him 'to carry you.' It's not easy, I can assure you, because silence frightens us and stillness seems like a waste of time to us. And yet the mystical life is silence and stillness 'in Him.'

Ciao little sister. Is your marriage with Him complete?

Pray for your brother

Carlo

33

Assekrem, Pentecost 1958

Ever dearest Dolce,

I'm staying in the Assekrem hermitage for a few days just of prayer and from here it is easy for me to run down and keep the appointment with you which you are surely expecting. I came up here to prepare myself for Pentecost and now my heart is singing. How sweet it is to meet the Bridegroom again! And even if the meeting is tinged with bitterness for past infidelities and misunderstandings, it always ends in the sweetest embrace which can be had on this Earth. The Holy Spirit is the bridegroom of the soul just as he was and is the bridegroom of Mary. He is the love of the Father and the Son made a Person, who comes to us poor creatures to give Himself totally and to demand the total gift of our selves. He is the very essence of God as Love who seeks us, wants us, speaks to us, loves us and seeks our possession.

And we resist Him, we betray Him and pass Him by indifferently.

How sad this all is!

And He patiently wins us over again with the strength of His mercy and presents us with the total sacrifice of Himself in Christ in order to draw us to Him with sighs too deep for words.

When oh when, Dolcidia, will we learn to love? When will we unfreeze our hearts of ice? When will we understand love? When will we stop judging? 'The Son of God came to save, not to judge the world,' and when will we unite ourselves to this redeeming Love?

I'd like to be near you, Dolcidia, to talk over with you these things which make up our vocation and the nub of all our activity here on Earth.

I have prayed for you over these special days and I would say that I have felt your prayer too. Here we are rather cut off during this period, given what is going on in the world. I have received a letter from home dated May 4th in which Mario tells me Mamma has had a new crisis. I would have liked to go to Italy both to see her again and to fulfil my electoral duty, but I really could not and cannot. The disturbances in Algiers and above all the worry of not being able to get back into Algeria put me off undertaking the journey. For the time being my place is here and I mustn't move.

Poor Mamma! How I feel for her now even in her shortcomings. Now I wouldn't like her to worry any more. And how painful it is for me to think that it has taken a whole lifetime to understand her fully. The mysteries of our sick human nature!

I've had no news from Italy for 20 days and she might well be dead by now. I can assure you, Dolce, that when I reach the Memorial of the dead I feel the need to say, 'Lord, if she is awaiting your Vision, give her your Kingdom.'

But the matter does not disturb me any more. I feel so much the union between Heaven and Earth that death no longer affects me: it is so natural to die in order to be There where our whole being will find peace, real peace. And what is more, I shall be sated with the very things which I have only been able to snatch at here: prayer and love.

In your last letter of April 25th you ask if I have received the pencils. Yes, I have received them and I had written thanking you. Which reminds me, you ask if I need anything else. Here it is, you could take on this job for me, 'stationery supplier'. If it is convenient for you, of course. Elastic bands, nibs, pins, all those little objects which are so useful for my daily work. Here I've got nothing but sand on my desk, which is an old packing case. Thanks and . . .

thanks to Mother Angela whom I remember *strongly* every day, especially in the run up to September. Ciao, Dolce. May God bless you and give you lots and lots of love for Him and for humanity.

Pray for me always and be sure of my love and remembrance.

Carlo

34

Tam, August 19th 1958

My dearest Dolce,

You are always good to me and even your complaint about my silence is a sign of goodness. You must forgive me as well because my current state of life sometimes excuses me. The tracks are not made for correspondence and when I get back I am so taken up with putting away the motor and the cargo that I forget anything else. I normally take advantage of the periods spent in the hermitage at Assekrem to write and I'm going up there next week. So . . . expect something. I have been meaning to write to Mother Angela for some time concerning the usual labour involved in the next Chapter in September, for which I have been praying for some time. I saw C. from the Salesians and I saw my old friend Mr Borra,[1] who has become a counsellor. If you see him, give him my regards.

And talking of illustrious Salesians, would you like to do me a favour?

In September I've got to stay some time at Assekrem studying a subject which is especially close to my heart. It's a theological subject with the following title: 'Immanence and Transcendence in God.'

I've little material here and I'm going to need some help, above all if I'm going to remain faithful to the most perfect Thomist orthodoxy.

You would have to telephone or seek out a professor of yours either from the Ateneo[2] or from the Rebaudengo[3] (Fr Camilleri,[4] for example) and ask him for some material. 15 pages of a text book would do me, or one chapter of a book which deals with the subject. Give it a go. I'm sure everyone will say yes to you. This is the subject, then: 'Immanence and Transcendence in God.' If you send it to me, I'll write you a doctorate on the spiritual life of a perfect Daughter of don Bosco.

All right?

I'm keeping the nice things back until next week.

For the time being I can only tell you that I'm fine, that where I'm staying everything is quiet, that Piero has written me a nice letter, that Lili is as silent as usual, that the Pope[5] has given a fine speech to Sisters who want to pray (the part about work is interesting, and on this subject don Bosco said some fine things), that the world no longer concerns me except as an object of prayer, that in September there will be a pilgrimage to Rome for Little Brothers on the occasion of the centenary of Charles de Foucauld's birth . . . and that I'll be staying here. Full stop.

I send you a warm hug.

Your Little Brother,

Carlo

35

Assekrem, August 28th 1958

Dearest Dolcidia,

As I told you in my last letter, I'm giving this week over to prayer and silence.

It's the good side of my present life: having opportunities for rest periods at Assekrem. To be sure, after my long journeys through the desert, staying here on this mountain for the sole purpose of prayer is delicious. I'd never leave here if I could, and that's a sign of the rightness of the life I lead. I who used to be thought a man of action am finding myself in solitude and silence.

I'm not sorry for it because the older I get the more I feel the value of the essential things and the relativity of everything.

My health is excellent and my leg is a touch better every day. my life is without problems, or at least has only one: that of union with God and in Him with His Mystical Body, the Church.

At the beginning of September many Little Brothers will gather in Rome. It's for a pilgrimage on the occasion of the centenary of the birth of Charles de Foucauld. I shall stay here and I assure you I do not envy those who are going. I feel so good here that I would willingly take a vow of stability in Africa. Don't be frightened: I think we'll see each other again. In any case it will be as God wills. I have written to Mother Angela on the occasion of the Chapter, offering my best wishes for this important gathering. You too will have a lot of work to do for this extraordinary event, and I will be with you all the way in constant prayer.

In your letter you tell me of the sense of impotence you feel about being what you would like to be. Dear Dolce, I think we've all got to go through this painful stage, except for the very rarest truly humble souls. It's our pride which has to be destroyed in us, our feeling of self-sufficiency (even for good), the idea that it's up to us to achieve our holiness. Since God can do nothing else to bring the point home, he lets us do all we can by ourselves. Then we begin to understand that by ourselves we are nothing and less than nothing. If on the other hand we could bring forth an act of real humility, everything would fall into place, and we would find that we had solved all our problems.

This is why the spirit of spiritual childhood is fundamental to the Kingdom of God and the 'sine qua non' condition of entry. The truly humble one is the child because it relies on itself for nothing but hopes for everything from its father and mother. My sister, do you want to run, to fly into the life of sanctity? *Then seek humility*, the real kind, that of Jesus, who although he was God 'did not think divinity a thing to be grasped at, but became a slave and died on a cross.'

I'm certain that the Lord leaves us in our sins and our infidelities for years and years (He who could heal us with a single communion) because He has no other way to humble us, to make us understand the terrible wretchedness of our proud souls.

Let us help one another along this way, little sister, with prayer and mortification.

Ciao. Have a good Chapter. I think the next time

you write to me you will be secretary to the Mother
General. Watch out!

Lots of kisses,

Carlo

36

Assekrem, October 8th 1958

Dearest Dolce,

Even though I confidently expected it, the splendid
news of the result of the Chapter gave me pleasure.
I know very few Mothers, but I know Mother Angela
and she is certainly one of God's souls. but there's
no point giving you my opinion: what matters is
to pray hard because the burden is heavy and the
responsibilities immense. Tell her that I will intensify
my prayers for her.

What about you? Are you staying with her or leaving? I'm eager to hear about it.

I've no news from home. Only one of the Brothers
returning from the pilgrimage to Rome tells me that
he found Liliana in bed.

I'm at Assekrem for two days after a four-day
'breakdown' I had on the road. I was left isolated
and alone with the Lord. I waited four days for the
car's spare part.

It's delightful to spend such a long period quite
alone, without books, without writing paper, obliged
to pray; it's . . . poor and naked prayer. It's then that
the finest discoveries are made because one ends up
by keeping quiet: *the principle of contemplation*

To keep quiet in prayer: how difficult it is! To bring the imagination, the tongue and the intelligence to silence: to keep quiet. To forbid oneself fine thoughts and bring oneself to an act of adoration like that of the host! Have you ever thought about the position of the Eucharist? It's the Incarnate Word's adoration of the Father. And how does He adore? In silence, by reducing Himself to zero, by abandoning Himself to sacrifice in love.

I think that there is the true model of prayer. At the beginning of our spiritual life, we feel the need in prayer to speak a lot, to say a lot (and that's right). But at a certain point, when real love wins us over, the highest prayer is silent adoration, accepting loving, abandoning ourselves to God's action without reserve.

How difficult it is, sister, to give up our busyness, even in holiness, to give up the helm and stay *waiting*, without making plans, without making any provision. Only in this way do we come to the certainty that it is God who must act and we must receive with love and self-sacrifice.

Thanks for the tremendous books you sent me: it's sound nourishment. I repeat my thanks (but I've already written to say so) for the very valuable stationery, which I hoard jealously. Thanks for everything.

Pray for your brother Carlo who loves you and carries you always in his heart.

Carlo

37

Assekrem, Christmas 1958

Dearest Dolce,

It's Christmas morning. Last night, after my annual spiritual exercises, I renewed my triennial vows. That means it's four years since I left Rome: one year at El Abiodh and three years divided between Berre and here in the Hoggar.

I'm not going to draw up an account of this period for you because I wouldn't know where to begin and, worse still, where to end. I can only tell you that I have found my way and that I am very happy.

I don't want to give you an apologia for the Little Brothers, *and in any case I don't believe in formulae any more*, but I just want to tell you that for four years I've lived in an atmosphere where the Gospel strikes a deeper chord, and that is all.

Here I'm left to get on with praying and my Superiors are more concerned about my holiness than with all my work. In short, I feel that what matters is the search for personal sanctity and union with God, not works.

And that's no small thing for a Congregation.

Yesterday evening a car arrived from Tamanrasset and I had the joy of receiving your last letter of December 15th.

I see that as usual you complain about my silence and I apologize profusely. You're not the only one left to complain about me.

It's strange, but throughout my life I have always found people eager to read what I write. It's really an act of great humility and patience and I thank them all, but I don't think I will change much.

On the mainland my old friends hunt about for news of me and I really can't understand why it matters to them. By now I'm a hermit and to a hermit time and space no longer exist. Don't you agree?

I'm not secretary to a Mother General; I live in a cave built out of stone and mud and I've little to tell.

The desert is always the same, the sky is always beautiful, the road deserted. What else can I say?

The only thing which is always new is God, but to talk about Him you've got to be a very good and careful secretary and even so you don't always get anything. What's more, He likes to present us with long periods of pure faith during which there's nothing for it but to be silent and strive to love, to love as much as you can with this old and stinking flesh, from which only iniquity and wretchedness can be squeezed.

What would you like to say?

But today my heart is full of Jesus and I could write you a novel. How many things the Lord told me last night! Especially *one* which I want to tell you about immediately.

Do you want the secret of everything? Do you want a boiled-down summary of the Gospel? Do you want a tiny, tiny, easy, easy formula for running, for flying onto the road to holiness?

Here it is:

'*Strive to love.*'

I don't tell you to love, because it's not an easy thing. *To love* certain unlikable 'Sisters' who are living and getting on alongside us, especially in a big house, is almost impossible. I tell you instead to 'strive' to love because translating a precept into action is almost always done *on the Cross*. Nothing which is really good and holy is easy for us. It takes an effort. It is the Cross laid upon our poor hearts and at the touch of it life begins to flow again.

Seek every day – I'm telling you my suggestions from last night – some opportunity to love more both God and Neighbour.

What results you'll see!

Jesus expects no more than that.

The whole of the Law and the Prophets is summed up as: *love – love*.

Try it and let me know.

In any case the advice does not come from me but from Jesus himself.

Tomorrow I shall come down off the mountain and take to the road again. I think I will carry on working here for the time being. I have asked Fr Prior if I may spend the rest of my life here, but I don't know what he will do with me.

In April, when the two years' work in my Society are up, I have a return air ticket paid for. It's for this reason that I said that I'm expecting to make a quick trip to Italy during 1959.

I wrote to Piero yesterday evening asking him whether his plans for 1959 include a little trip. We could arrange a meeting. But I don't know anything definite yet.

I've no great news from Rome. I have just one rich memory of John XXIII. One day when I was passing through Paris he invited me to lunch at the Nunciature. When I left I had stomach ache. The reason certainly wasn't the food served, on the contrary. . . . *but the laughing which he'd made me do.*

A Pope who can make people laugh and knows

how to laugh himself is a great sign of trust in Providence. Don Bosco was a fine example.

Don't you think so? Ciao little sister. I send you a warm hug.

Carlo

Thanks for the stationery. Magnificent!

38

Tam, Easter 1959 (March 29th)

Dearest Dolce and dearest Emerenziana,

It's Easter and I feel so happy. Never have I felt Jesus our Redeemer alive in my soul as I do now. In this solitude of the heart and spirit the mysterious knowledge of God becomes ever livelier and more personal, while the world increasingly slackens its grip on a soul immersed in silence and fed on poverty.

How true it is, sisters, that the whole drama of existence unfolds in this live relationship with God, who in His wonderful plans decided to make us actors in this live, since it takes two to make love.

The schemes of the world and the agitations of people are nothing, a nothingness which leaves a void, unhappiness, remorse; what remains is love and love alone.

I would have liked to write to you earlier, my dear sisters, but I couldn't. My companion on the road has eye trouble and had to leave for France, leaving me alone with the work. In this way the trip I had already planned for myself *has been put back until God should want, it could easily be autumn or even later*. But that's all right and I'm not complaining.

The only thing which prompted the trip was the situation at home, to which I would willingly have given a little time to reach a solution.

But if God did not want it so, it means that He could do without me and I go back to trusting in Him and . . . in you. I only take it upon myself to tell you my thoughts, which naturally are not commands but just have the force of advice.

God says in Genesis that when a marriage takes place, '*A man leaves his father and mother and joins himself to his wife, and the two become one body.*' The thought is straightforward and sets us on the way to a solution to the problem. The married couple – normally – should leave home to set up a new home. This makes things infinitely easier.

The patriarchal family, in which everybody used to stay together, or still does, is the source of a lot of problems. As far as is possible, this is not what should be established.

It seems harsh to talk like that and yet it is the most opportune way to retain and strengthen affection. An Arab proverb says, 'Keep the tents apart and the hearts close,' and it's very true.

When we are under one another's feet, when we are forced to live too close together; *instead of being an advantage it injures love*.

After all, we have clear proof of it right in our own home and if – immediately after her marriage – Lili had gone away, *the love between the two families would have been stronger and heaps of harsh words would have been avoided*. We Italians are still bound to a strange

sentimentality which ends up by harming us and
which puts us in certain situations which are poison-
ous for daily life.

You will say: the problem remains of giving assistance to parents, especially when they are old, but
what is not said is whether that assistance is worthwhile when it helps to make them grumble from
morn till night.

'Leave them alone': this is the first great assistance;
'leave them in peace' in their habits and their tastes.

Material assistance is indeed needed too, but that
will sort itself out by visiting them from time to time
and getting a good domestic help for them.

You will say: 'What a disgrace for a daughter to
get domestic help for her parents,' and I will reply:
'When Mamma married and left her home she did
no more than her duty.' Imagine what it would have
been like if she had stayed with her old folks! How
would she have looked after her children and her
husband?

Believe me, sisters, it's not cruel to leave the old
folks behind when one marries: it's natural, it's the
route desired by God. Cruelty would be leaving them
without food or affection, but it isn't cruel to go away
in order to follow one's own vocation. And a vocation is
not just becoming a priest or religious, but also getting married.

So my opinion is this. Papà and Mamma are to
stay alone in the old apartment on the Via Aurelia.
Lili and her husband are to go and look for another
small apartment, preferably close to Mario's work. A
domestic help is to be looked for who will help every
day with the housework, and you will see that everything will be peaceful again. Instead of screaming at

Lili or Mario all day long, Mamma will find complete peace and perfect calm. *The house on the Via Aurelia will remain the common home where you, I, Lili, Piero, etc., etc. will go from time to time to visit our parents for as long as Providence in its love shall leave them on Earth.*

Take my advice and you will see that everything will work out better. It's natural – in answer to Dolce's question – that the money from my pension should go first of all to the old folks. That's the first duty of children. All right? I'll wait to hear what you think.

Kisses,

Carlo

39

Tam, August 18th 1959

Dearest Dolce,

If everything goes well and the aeroplane stops here, I shall leave for Algiers and then for Marseilles. I don't know yet when I will get to Rome, but I think it will not be later than September 1st.

As regards your absence from Turin, I don't think there's anything to worry about. In any case, I shall pass through there on the way back towards France, therefore after September 20th. So we shall be able to meet.

As regards the worries about which you wrote, I have to tell you that I found your letter not a little mortifying. Basically, it convinced me that you remain completely fixed in your own opinions and that not even basing myself on exact quotations from Sacred Scripture is of any use when convictions are mistaken to the core.

I shall not tell Papà and Mamma that Lili 'did well to go away,' I shall say only that it was her right if in conscience she felt that continuing to stay could *damage her union with her husband*.

You see, Dolce, what you have not understood is this: when a couple marry they take on new *duties*, and the *first* duty is to follow the husband. Now it certainly isn't Lili who wanted to leave, *but it is her husband*.

What was left for the poor girl to do? Either she fell out with her husband and created a rift, or she accepted. Her duty was to accept even with suffering, and that is what she has done. Therefore to speak of betrayal is at the very least offensive.

Did you perhaps 'betray' when you left home to become a Salesian?

I think that you are convinced that you have done God's will, otherwise you would not have taken this step. Well, Lili found herself in the same position because marriage is a vocation too, whether you like it or not. Rest assured, sister, that there are mistakes which need correcting in the way marriage is conceived of *in Piedmont*, because they are the cause of no little harm.

At any rate, keep calm, I shall not make Papà and Mamma suffer, I will not enter into discussions, I will assist them all the way, I will try to help them as I've always helped them because, until proved wrong, I have kept them closer to me than all my other brothers and sisters who argue at a distance but who do not remember *that the burden of assistance*

*falls on them too and it would not be out of the question
to request* their Congregations for a year each to be
with their parents at a difficult time.

And don't wave the Rule at me, because charity is
above all and the problem can be solved perfectly
well, if there is the will to do so.

A transfer to Turin could also be considered – if
your health still allows – but the problem cannot be
embittered with useless recriminations against Lili
and Mario.

So until we meet, with every willingness to be
useful to our loved ones.

Love,

Carlo

40

Tam, November 16th 1959

Dearest Dolce,

My arrival in Tam was marked by a heap of worries
and work due to my long absence. I have had the
comfort of your letters and I have thanked the Lord
because this last meeting of ours has strengthened
our already great affection.

It has been a real gift from God, both because of
the time spent close to Papà and Mamma in Rome
and because of our really deep understanding.

Don't be too amazed at Lili. She didn't even write
to me for my name day. And to think that I had sent
her a present a few days earlier . . . she will get
round to it.

Papà and Mamma have written me an affectionate letter. As regards the 'burial site' you have done well. Let us carry on down the same path and together we will sort the matter out.

You ask in two of your letters for me to write something about the spirit of faith and about obedience. I shall do so for you at the right moment, when the inspiration takes me. but in the meantime I want to send you some writings by Fr Voillaume, much profounder than anything I could do. You won't have any difficulty translating from the French. They are fantastic. I only ask you to send them back to me when you've finished with them. You will find great wealth also in the book *Seeds of the Desert*. Get it out and read it carefully: you will see.

Courage, sister, along with faith and love.

Love,

Carlo

41

Tam, December 2nd 1959

Darling Dolce,

Thanks for your letter, even though it did not contain good news. I wrote home immediately in the hope that Emerenziana is still there.

Mother Angela has been truly good and I have admiration for her motherly gesture. What is more, she is always true to herself: I have always known her to be like that, and it is her greatness. I will write to her immediately to thank her, as you want me to.

I've also received the vitamins and I'm grateful to you: I've enough for a year at least. After that I hope to get them directly from Italy where – I think I can say so – I think I shall be within a year.

Don't concern yourself too much about Lili and Mario, just pray calmly and peacefully. Drive out all thought of rejection which might spring up in your heart.

Certainly it is difficult for you to understand certain attitudes: better then not even to try to understand. It's another world, which I do understand and which does not amaze me.

It's the yawning gap which separates two generations into armed camps.

Your job – believe me – is just to pray. After all, that's what you know how to do and which you do with such exactitude and verve.

I have confidence both in Lili and Mario. The one really positive thing is that they love one another. You can be sure of it. When you're with them just 'pretend' to understand them, to have high regard for them. More than that, try to love them. Love – as you know – is the great force, perhaps the only one, which overcomes every obstacle.

More than that you cannot do.

Dislike is mutual and has to be overcome with patience and good will.

Thanks for what you told me about our last meeting. God, I hope, will grant us more and better meetings if we are faithful to Him.

I could do with a few more end-of-year supplies. This is what I'm short of: writing paper like this, some envelopes, sticking plaster, aspirin, next year's calendars.

Be brave, sister. May God make your heart burn
for love of Him alone.

We shall write to each other again before Christmas
when I renew my vows.

I send you a big hug.

Love,

Carlo

42

Tam, Christmas 1959

Dear Dolce,

I have finished my spiritual exercises and would
have a whole book to write to you. But the material
is still tumbling around my head and even more so
in my heart and I absolutely cannot tell you the things
I would like to communicate to you. Let me think
about them a bit longer.

If you're in a hurry, read St John of the Cross's
book: *The Ascent of Mount Carmel*. Those are the
things I want to tell you.

I'm happy, sister, so happy, despite my tribu-
lations. God is so good and so great!

And yet, so as not to crush us with His greatness
he presented Himself to us as a weak and defenceless
baby. What an immense mystery of love Christmas
is! When will we understand it fully?

I pray a lot for you and you should pray for your
Carlo. I am pleased that Emerenziana is in Rome and
I hope she will enjoy this period as a grace from God.

Mamma is happy and . . . doesn't even argue any

more. I enclose a letter from the mother of an old student of mine. Get her to call and talk to her. She will explain her situation to you. I think it might interest you. Who knows whether a good work might not come out of it!

I send you a big hug.

Love,

Carlo

43

Tam, January 15th 1960

Dearest Dolce,

The fourth parcel which you were good enough to send me arrived yesterday evening and so I can let you know that everything is fine. The first two (stationery) arrived much earlier, but that is not to be wondered at given the irregularity of the service at Christmas time.

Thanks for everything: I am stocked up again for at least a year, and after that . . . as God wills.

I have no fresh news from home but I hope it's good. Piero wrote to me from San Francisco, and I think it will not be long before he arrives in Italy. I would be happy to see him come here to make his retreat, but I fear he will not find the time. It would be lovely for him to spend a period in Africa – he is so taken up by his concerns!

If you can, insist, because I feel he needs it. In his letters he is much more preoccupied than when he was a simple priest. I know the temptations of power and . . . being a Bishop is to be prey to such things.

My life carries on for the best. I'm spending a really good period in the company of St John of the Cross who really is the king of the mystics and the master of the life of prayer.

My health is excellent and I have to say that the month I spent in Italy really did do me good. And yet this Africa is so marvellous! Believe me, just thinking about leaving here makes me feel sad.

It will be as God wills: I have entrusted my affairs to Him.

Thanks for the confectionery and even more for the lovely pictures and for the magnificent 'Angelus Domini'.

You are really kind to your brother. I haven't received so much as a sweet from Lili in 5 years. You see how patient one has to be with the young. And to say that at the end of it they still feel themselves to be *victims*. What a sad sickness. Victimization is truly a cancer of the soul from which it is difficult to be healed!

Seeing that you're so good to me, I'm going to ask you another favour.

When I'm out on the road I come into contact with drivers and mechanics: people used to the desert who for months on end are away from home and away from the sacraments.

When they see me, they always ask me for medals or things of that kind to hang on the car or put next to the clock. Basically, they are good signs of Christianity and it's good to satisfy them. For example, I gave your 'Angelus Domini' this morning to a mechanic who has not seen his wife for six months.

He cried with joy because it was the most beautiful gift he could wish to send to his wife who he told me said the rosary for him every day.

And so to my conclusion: when you find religious objects of this kind in cupboards (medals, pendants, key-rings), send them to me and I assure you that you will be contributing to doing good in Africa as well. Naturally they've got to be presentable because otherwise it wouldn't be good to have horrible objects reminding us of God and the Virgin Mary.

The French here have some, but they are in such poor taste that I carefully avoid giving them.

Thanks.

I've nothing else to tell you for the time being.

Have you seen the programme on television about the Little Brothers?[1] Perhaps you've heard it spoken of? It was filmed here in the Sahara.

Ciao, sister. May God enkindle you with His love and make you little like Baby Jesus.

Pray for me and I'll pray for you every day.

I send you a very warm hug.

                                                    Carlo

44

Tam, February 10th 1960

Dearest Dolce,

Thanks for the little gold mine of religious objects which you sent me. You cannot imagine how precious and useful they are to me, and how many people they will make happy. Here in the Sahara there's nothing, nothing – only sand – and these little things are deeply appreciated.

Thanks to you and thanks naturally to your great Mother Angela. She gets greater all the time.

I have written home sending the first instalment of a sum Papà should pay to decorate the house.

I have received a letter from Emerenziana: very very good.

Everything is calm here. Don't be frightened by the riots in Algiers. In the desert peace reigns supreme. It seems that the French are about to explode an atomic bomb, but we are far enough away to be calm. After all, it will be more of a little propaganda bomb than anything else. They have a need to think they're still *great*. Human weakness!

I'll be thinking about you in your joy at seeing Piero again. Tell him to retain his 'littleness,' his spiritual childhood. That he should not think too much of the 'hardware' he wears on his cassock. After all it counts for nothing. The only worthwhile privilege is the 'privilegium crucis'. The rest is nothing.

Love,

Carlo

45

Tam, Ash Wednesday 1960 (March 2nd)

Dear Dolce,

Just a couple of lines to thank you for your last letter, in which you tell me of Piero's stopover in

Turin. Now I'm waiting for something from Rome, but it will be slower coming. In any case, good. I'm happy at what you wrote to me about our poor, tired, ill-dressed brother. It's good that way. I have no great love for decked up priests and bishops on the look out for hand-kissing. This is the reason why I worry about my brother being a bishop.

Your vitamins are doing me a lot of good: you guessed well.

Yesterday evening I made some drivers happy with your religious objects. Thanks again.

I'm well and happy even if life is hard.

I wish you a Happy Lent 1960.

I shall spend it here at Tam.

I'll write to you at greater length soon. At the moment I've got to go out straightaway.

A big hug from your Little Brother

(Carlo)

46

Tam, Easter 1960 (April 17th)

Dearest Dolce,

I'm especially close to you this Easter 1960.

Our Lady of Sorrows has presented me with the gift of my fiftieth birthday and I cannot tell you the sweetness of its passing. It was an extraordinary thing and I had the feeling that while navigating the harsh sea of life my feet had touched firm ground.

In your letter you ask me to explain to you the meaning of this harshness and you ask yourself whether it depends on the road or the sand or something else.

Dear Dolce, I have the impression that the Lord is cradling you in sweetness.

At the age of 50 the spiritual life is bitter. What St John of the Cross says about the dark night of the senses and the dark night of the spirit is true, and it is a dogma of faith that there is no arriving at our Resurrection with Christ without passing through death.

And death is death, and it's not comfortable.

To die every day is a terrible thing, it's a Calvary, and I think that Jesus Himself has pity on this human race of ours as we die, caught between the fogginess of a limited faith and the sadness of a hope which is even more limited and exacting.

Don't you agree?

In Gethsemane Jesus Himself 'began to be afraid and anxious'. Do you understand? – Afraid and anxious – and he had a quite different makeup from ours, wrapped as it is in an experience of sin and weakness.

I believe that we ought to have a lot of compassion for humanity (including our own). We are so fragile, so little, so nothing. And if we are to be saved, it is certainly not by our own efforts but only by the infinite and most sweet love of Jesus our Redeemer.

And then, why should the life of Jesus be so harsh, so abandoned, so tragic, and ours different?

Recite the 'Stabat Mater' every day and you will see what a casket of sorrows passed into the Heart of that human being who was so pure and close to God, Mary.

So there you have explained the reason for the

harshness of my life, even if – I assure you – it is nothing compared to what I deserve and what I owe.

After July I'll tell you my programme for next year, that is, whether I shall stay here or return to Italy. I don't know yet.

A warm greeting to Mother Angela, always present in my heart, and a hug to you.

Love,

Carlo

47

Meryem-Ana,[1] January 10th 1961

My dearest Dolce,

I wanted to spend a bit more time with you talking over the great events of the recent past, both to thank you and to thank the Lord, who as ever is extremely merciful.

I didn't think I would suffer the way I have over Mamma's death.[2] The death of a mother, I think, is always a unique event for someone on earth, and it shakes us to the core. Then there's a mystery there, more than I realized. I thought I knew Mamma, and yet I did not: it seems to me as though I've only now discovered her: it takes death to bring out the whole truth, both about ourselves and our neighbours.

I would very much have liked to be with her at the end. I had promised her that and she wanted it a lot. Instead the Lord has required of me a much greater and more heroic stripping and solitude: that of the Virgin Mary after the death of Jesus. Think, Dolce, of the suffering to which Our Lady was subjected after the death of her son: to go on living and to live apart from Him. Living on pure faith and reliving the tragedy of Calvary day after day!

We are not called to all of that, but we do not escape our share of solitude, of abjection, in short of death. Do we?

And yet I believe that it is *there* that life is at its most profound, that precisely in death there lives the root of the little good we can do on this Earth. When Jesus on Calvary cried out, 'Father, why have you abandoned me?,' he lived through the unspeakable agony of his mysterious dark night of the spirit, and did a great deal more for the redemption of the world than when he preached or performed miracles.

Suffering is the great treasure of life, especially when it is spiritual suffering, mature and solitary, lightened a little at a time. Everything else is like a preparation, but altogether more superficial, light and unsubstantial. The years of human fullness pass by and we leave no trace, but in the passing of these few minutes we build eternity.

Courage, Dolce. You know how much I love you and how close I feel to you. Let us pray in Mamma's words, 'Virgin Mary, help me!' It really is like that, and it's a summary of all prayer. Until we meet in a month and a half, I send you a hug.

Love,

Carlo

48

St Gildas, August 10th 1961

Dearest Emerenziana, dearest Dolce,

Eight days ago this evening I began my retreat, which will continue without interruption until September 3rd and will be taken up again (this time preached) on the 7th at Farlete[1] in Spain, ending on the 15th with the taking of perpetual vows.[2].

As you can sée, I am committed to a battle which is neither short nor easy, but I am sure that, with the help of God and your prayers, I shall succeed this time in taming this terribly stubborn mule.

This place is extremely suitable: real desert, as is our tradition. On a Normandy crag, battered by Atlantic storms, there are some little hermitages: every hermitage consists of a tiny cell and an adjoining little chapel in which Jesus is present. So we live in twos: He and this poor devil of a neighbour, who has to make the effort to watch and pray, not an easy thing when one is lazy and stiff-necked.

We are completely cut off, and shall remain so for a month. The Brothers who live on the nearby island come to bring us food like the ravens to St Benedict and Elijah. The Farlete retreat on the other hand will be in common and preached by Fr Prior (after six years of religious life, these will be the first sermons! As you can see we are not profligate with words!).

But this is the schooling for Brother Carlo of Jesus: if you want to pray, the Lord is all you need.

To tell you that I'm happy is too little and you understand me well. The Lord has led me from one realm to another by roads which were not easy; he has delivered me when I was in danger, pushed me, pulled me, carried me. He surely could not have done any more with a mule like me. But now there is no going back for me, especially because I feel the goal is in sight.

Half an hour ago I was doing some adoration and I said to Jesus: You who see Mamma, tell her to help me; tell her that I'm praying for her, but she should pray for me and give me a good heaven.

I had the impression that Jesus was pleased that I talked to him about Mamma! He too loved his Own.

Now I'm telling you too, because after Mamma you're the closest to me: pray, heave hard. If I make it, if I get there to Him, I'll give you a hand too! Life on this Earth is a roped-together climbing party and charity is its bond.

You can write to me here at St Gildas. Yesterday I received Emerenziana's lovely letter with the fresh news. In a month or two I shall receive Liliana's, but I'm used to this. Don't laugh, Dolce! And don't make useless comparisons!

A big hug for you both,

Carlo

49

St Gildas, August 25th 1961

Dearest Dolce,

I've just received your letter with your news and . . . your concern about Moncalvo. Thanks for everything, as usual.

I'm finishing my labours as a hermit. It's been sweet but harsh, beautiful but bitter, enchanting but severe.

I leave here on the morning of the 4th to be in my new residence on the evening of the 6th:

Farlete (Saragossa)

Spain

where with other Brothers I shall make my vows on September 15th. So you know where to find me. After the 15th, I hope to be able to leave immediately. If there are no difficulties . . . of obedience I would like to be in Rome on the 18th to speed up the most urgent matters. Then I shall fly out to my destination.

I'm no prophet, but I have the impression that my base will be a Brotherhood near Marseilles (that famous adoration Brotherhood which Father wants me to found for him). From there I will have charge of matters in Italy and therefore a quick trip there from time to time. These are my guesses. Soon will come the decisions and obedience.

Things being the way they are, I don't think I can take on Moncalvo. You know the way things are. The superior needs to know at least the exact dates and I . . . cannot give her them. What can I do on the eve of my vows?

Tell her then this time to look for other preachers. For my part, if I'm in Italy I will be very happy to return to Moncalvo,[1] even for more than a day trip. But for the regular spiritual exercises make arrangements with others.

Thanks for the commission. I need to reduce my correspondence, which unfortunately is always heavy, especially during retreats.

I send you a hug, sure of having you close to me at the altar on September 15th.

Love,

Carlo

50

Marseilles, February 6th 1962

Dearest,

I have just received your letter and I'm writing back immediately because I detect in it a certain concern about me. No, my dear: working with cows and manure[1] is no loss but a gain. It's *a calm world, at peace and relaxed, because it's natural, and anything natural is in God*. I'm really very happy and I beg you to believe me. I don't get too tired: would to God that I were more generous! Nor do the Brothers make me suffer: don't worry, to be sure, our life is serious, far from any middle class frills, but it is quite the reverse of unbearable. And then: *it is and remains* in the truth and *in love* and this is very important. We make a real effort to love one another, to walk together, to help each other in the spiritual life. Being in the Brotherhood is a great help to me, even if it costs me something and it is necessary to become little at all costs.

Here the respected and heeded professor Carretto does not exist; instead there's Little Brother Carlo, old and lame, who can be rebuked by any newcomer and who must live his hidden life like Jesus in Nazareth.

Believe me, sister: *what is sweet on a human level is rarely constructive and often dangerous on a divine level; what is bitter on a human level is precious in the eyes of God.*

Thank God that I have become a Little Brother. I could find no better school for becoming little, humble and silent. From this viewpoint the Brotherhood is the most precious discipline for understanding something about the spiritual life.

Thanks for everything, sister. Pray for me and I shall pray for you: life is the light, and we must hasten our death by dying first as living beings, so that real death will find us already corpses and will no longer frighten us.

When you come to Marseilles, you will come to see my Brotherhood. You'll like it. A big hug,

Carlo

51

Marseilles, Holy Saturday 1962 (April 21st)

My dearest,

Thanks again for what you did for me on my last trip. You were particularly . . . sweet. I enclose the paper for your colleague.

This Easter of '62 is a particularly *happy* one for me. God is giving me a lot of special comfort. I have asked Him to let me spend these last years of my life in His love, making me understand and live out His redemptive suffering. I know that everything depends on humility, and I know that if the Lord does not grant me this grace it is because of the pride which nullifies His gift, or rather . . . makes the situation worse.

We are so sick!

Courage, Dolce, and press onwards. I can tell you that Jesus loves you a lot and could make you a great saint. The difficulty remains . . . becoming little, little in our ideas, little in our estimation of ourselves, little in our hearts.

A big affectionate kiss,

Carlo

52

Marseilles, May 6th 1962

Dearest,

Thanks for the lovely multiple telephone call!

I'm sending you your fellow-sister's letter and you should send me her name and surname so that I can correspond regularly. I'll send her a fine consolatory epistle!

Things are good here.

The Lord is making me His day by day. His intimacy is so sweet.

I want to reach the point of *being with Him always*, of no longer feeling any difference between being in church and being out at work: of adoring Him continually even in the midst of the bustle of the daily round.

Ciao dear sister,

Carlo

53

Marseilles, Feast of St Anne 1962

Dearest,

Your very dear letter arrived this morning with Papà's enclosed. Our old boy has found his paradise at Isola.[1] So much the better. The more I think about it and the more time passes, the more I see how meeting Anna was help from Heaven. Even the summer holidays have been solved.

I'm pleased about your travels. There's so much to learn from meeting other people!

I see that you have discovered that the richest people are the coldest in spiritual matters.

That's how it is, and Jesus had already said it: 'Woe to the rich!'

The world and the Cross do not get along too well together and comfort and holiness do not share the same room, even in us.

Isn't that true?

I therefore hope that the Daughters of Mary Help of Christians will always *stay* poor, really poor.

And may my sister also always remain as poor and good as she is now.

All right?

A big hug for you and a warm greeting for Mother Angela.

Love,

Carlo

54

Marseilles, September 5th 1962

Dear little sister,

I am with you as you undertake the spiritual Exercises during these days. This letter of mine will reach you as you are taking up the normal rhythm of your life again.

God has always had a special love for you and gave you a strong balanced nature, an aptitude for work, ease in relationships and goodwill. All these gifts have gone with you always and you have certainly built up merit.

Now begins the last stage, which is that of stripping away. It is the most important stage, because it ends in the total sacrifice of ourselves, as it is for Jesus in the Mass.

Stripping ourselves is not easy. It's a question of giving up the gifts which are dear to our personality, and it's natural they should be so.

Memory and strength fail, feelings cool, the will weakens. Sometimes we have the impression of being just a *nothing*.

And yet this is the moment of utmost love, the moment when the Beatitudes live in us.

When Jesus says, 'Blessed are the poor, blessed are those who weep,' he does not just mean the poverty of money or the weeping of suffering. He means above all the state of poverty which is that of the human soul: '*it is a nothing*', it is truly poor in everything. And if it weeps it is precisely because it feels that, being so poor, it cannot offer God anything except its 'nothingness'.

There is no moment in our life which is more sublime, there is no revelation which is more profound. It is truth in the absolute. We are nothing. God is everything.

And so, dear sister, I wish you well as you tackle this last stretch on your journey with the soul of someone who is *poor*.

Don't be amazed if you experience dryness, emptiness, loneliness and wretchedness: these are the corollaries of poverty, they are the foretaste of contemplation. This contemplation is nothing less than the breath of divine life enclosed in this nothing which is the human soul.

I'll pray for you and you are to pray for your poor Carlo who loves you.

Carlo

55

November 5th 1962

Dear Dolce,

Here's my new address for you:

Petit frère de Jesus
St Laurent de Neste[1] (Hautes Pyrénées)

It's a little place in the Pyrenees very near to Lourdes and similar in that it's, poor, simple, mountainous and green.

I'm really at peace as I wanted and I think I will do well here.

I thought I would be staying a few more days in Marseilles but instead I had to bring forward my arrival.

So much the better.

I'll write to you at greater length, but for the time being I'm taken up with getting the Brotherhood going, given that I'm also the Superior here.

I love you and send you a hug,

Carlo

56

St Laurent, November 25th 1962

My dearest sister,

I was thinking about you returning to Turin after your break in Rome, which was lovely I am sure.

The setting up of the new Brotherhood is finished. Once again the Lord looked after things and I can assure you that I'm enchanted by it. The village of St Laurent is in a river valley, 'the Neste'. It is a perfect image of Lourdes, with its mountains and its peace. Life is still fairly old-fashioned, with cow pastures and poor houses. The surroundings – even if they have changed – are those in which Bernadette lived, and it's lovely, lovely, lovely.

The Pyrenees are poor, poorer than the Alps, but they retain a very special simplicity and peace. I think I shall have an excellent period here, praying. And I need it.

In one of your last letters you said you were worried about me, that you had noticed something new in me. It may be, my dear, that the Lord is preparing something new for me. It is certain that I have felt as never before that earthly life no longer matters to me. These are difficult things to talk about. It's not that I don't value God's gift contained in every twenty-four hours of life down here, but . . . it seems I have grasped something else and the horizon down here no longer attracts me the way it used to do. I seem to have run my course.

But we shall see.

I've also got another reason for feeling 'Nunc dimittis': the historic importance of the Council. I have longed so much for twenty years that something should come about in the Church to change things! I have really suffered. And now I think that it has happened, that Spring is knocking at the door, that the polemic between the Church and the world is silent for a moment, that the oldest and most reactionary situations are opening up and . . . so many other things are happening!

What happiness, my sister!

And how true it is that it is God who acts, not us.

Who would have thought of such a thing at the close of Pius XII's pontificate? It was the Almighty preparing the ground for future sowing.

So . . . don't worry! I'm not depressed. Instead I'm more aware than I used to be, more at peace, but as though on the eve of something, and you know that vigil vestments are not white or red, but *purple*.

You want the telephone number? Here it is: St Laurent de Neste 17. It's the number of the Parish Priest, who's already a close friend. However, I wouldn't like to bother him too much, given that the Brotherhood is several hundred yards away from the presbytery. What shall we do? Would it be possible to fix a time? All the more so since a call every fortnight or so would be enough. What do you think of that?

The shirts duly arrived. It was a lovely gift. Thanks to you and the Sisters at Moncalvo. I have sent a little thank-you to Sr Elsa.

I have received a fine letter from Piero and have written back to him. I was in a jolly mood. Emerenziana has written too. Our sister is always such a darling!

I'm really happy about Papà. This period is a gift from God, it's clear to see.

Who can tell what will await me when the office on the Via Aurelia in Rome is open!?![1]

Anything could happen.

For the time being I want to spend a good period of adoration here at St Laurent, close to Our Lady.

Do you agree?

I send you a hug with lots of love.

Your Little Brother,

Carlo

57

St Laurent, December 10th 1962

Dearest,

This morning I had the pleasure of hearing you again and of hearing about Piero's programme. I'm therefore writing to thank you and to give you a ticket for Piero.

I hope then to be able to greet Piero by telephone next Thursday. In any case two greetings are not too many.

I was in Lourdes on December 8th to spend the day for the feast of the Immaculate Conception.

I'm finally getting ready for my annual spiritual exercises, which I shall make from December 26th to the beginning of January.

Get ready . . . to help me with your notepaper and your prayer. After your telephone call I heard Papà's voice. If it was on the telephone, it means he had already got out of bed. I was pleased because I was a bit worried.

I'm happy with what's happening at the Council in Rome.

Behind the 'hullabaloo' of the Bishops, who some-times no longer know what they're fishing for, we can clearly sense the action of the Holy Spirit.

It's wonderful!

We must pray hard, because God is truly with us at this time!

Love,

Carlo

58

St Laurent, February 8th 1963

My dearest Dolce,

You're always wanting long, spiritual, etc., etc. letters and I'm always eager to send them to you.

I've thought of something; I'll write for you and

with you a book I've had in mind for some time:
Letters from the Desert.[1]

I'll send it to you chapter by chapter. You can
read it, type it up and send it back to me with your
comments.

We shall see what comes of it. It may be that you
will publish it after my death, if it pleases God. At
any rate, here's the introduction for you.

I don't know if you can trace two of my articles for
me, one on prayer and the other called, 'Under the
Great Rock'. The first was published in *L'Osservatore
Romano*,[2] the other in the Rome *Crociata missionaria*.[3]
They would be useful to me. I have received your
last letter with the article from *Oggi*[4] about Gedda's[5]
marriage.

Thanks for everything, but most of all for your
love.

Love,

(Carlo)

59

St Laurent, March 1st 1963

Dear Dolce,

Here are the first two chapters for you: enjoy yourself thinking about me under the great rock.

I have agreed to give a lecture to the university
students of Turin on May 2nd. It will be after the
election and I count on seeing you again then. I shall
also go to Vercelli to visit Emerenziana.

Things are good here, even if the winter is long.

But Jesus warms my heart for me.

Carlo

60

St Laurent, March 10th 1963

Dear Dolce,

Here are the chapters on prayer for you. They are the heart of my little book and have cost me quite a lot.

Basically, they are a summary of the whole of my life as it now stands and – if it should please God – they will help anyone to seek out the road to intimate prayer with God.

We are working to finish our little chapel, which is to be consecrated by the Bishop of Lourdes[1] on March 21st. It will be dedicated to St Joseph.

For the rest, peace and joy in the Lord.

Love,

Carlo

61

St Laurent, March 27th 1963

My dear Dolce,

I have proceeded to make the corrections you suggested. Not for nothing have I named you the 'reviser' of my book. Here then are two more chapters for you: 'You Are Nothing' and 'Who Guides the World?'

The Lord is visibly helping me, and if it were not so I really would not be in the mood for writing.

I'm putting it in two envelopes because the postage costs less. The numbering of both the chapters and the pages will all be done by hand, don't worry . . .

I see that you are a good and accurate typist. I had the joy of hearing Lili on the telephone. I was pleased: she is in good form and I feel that Mario is getting on well too.

Praise God!

Thanks for your prayers. We have to hurry the pace because we are at the end. We need to reach a great union with God, a great peace day and night, a life of adoration even when writing or sweeping the floor . . .

I send you a big hug.

Carlo

62

St Laurent, April 2nd 1963

Dearest Dolce,

53 years ago I saw the light of this world. My thoughts of gratitude go first to God and then to my dear Mamma, who will surely think of making a little gift of prayer for me today. She will say at least a rosary for me, won't she?

It's certain it won't be forgotten, not by her!

Thanks for your good wishes and for Emerenziana's. Yesterday I received that of E. and that of Piero along with your letter.

Not bad, is it?!

Thanks also for the work you are doing for me. It seems to me it's getting on well.

It's certain that the Lord is helping me quite a lot and is urging me to finish. If it were not for that I would not even have got started: and He knows it.

As regards the house, the surveyor is quite right. There's no problem about the repairs. Tell Papà he can draw the money from my Rome account. That way he will have no worries. Or alternatively, you can take it out of the increase in rent. In six months everything will be fixed. Do as you wish, I have no problem of that kind provided our dear old Papà is left in peace.

I will try to obey your request to have a happy birthday.

Love,

                                                  Carlo

63

St Laurent, April 17th 1963

Dearest Dolce,

Here are three more chapters. We have completed more than two-thirds of the book.

Re-reading your typescripts, I admire your exactness.

It's not easy with my 'symbolic' writing.

All is peace and serenity here. I do however have a sick Brother who worries me a little.

You ask me about Mamma. I feel she is very near and in Paradise. Only rarely do I still mention her name at the 'memento', but I often think about her in prayer and in faith.

You know what it's like with faith: you know everything and you know nothing; it's darkness, but it's a bright darkness. It's the greatest wonder of our relationship with God!

As regards the house, I agree. Thanks for the rules governing electoral journeys and for all the information.

Papà and Anna have written to me apologizing, poor things, for having forgotten my birthday. There's really no reason with a scatterbrain like me. Don't you agree? How many of them have I forgotten in my life!

As regards the young lady and your brother-in-law I will do my best, you know. However, I've always got to wait for the inspiration which . . . does not always match the haste and eagerness of Miss [. . .]. You know?!

Love,

Carlo

64

St Laurent, May 8th 1963

Dear Dolce,

These four chapters bring the labour of my book to an end.

In the chapter on Nazareth I have included a quotation from Gandhi, but from memory, not having the text to hand.

You will have to do me a favour (and so have the opportunity to read the book, which is extremely good). Get a copy from the bookshop, pub. La Locusta, of the slim volume *Writings of Gandhi*.[1]

It's a very interesting little work. You will easily find the quotation and so can quote it fully.

Thanks!

I have received the letter from Sister Delespaul. I'm grateful to you. I shall reply to Lili.

Things are fine here. The cold is over and Spring has come.

On Sunday I'm going to Lourdes and I shall remember you especially.

A big greeting to Sister Giovanna and all my respects to Mother Angela.

I send you a warm hug,

Carlo

65

St Laurent, June 22nd 1963

My dearest Dolce,

I'm pleased that you have felt all the greatness of John XXIII, and you are quite right that if we were still in the early Church he would be canonized by popular acclaim.

I feel it deep in my heart and I feel that he helps me a lot: *he was a great saint.*[1]

Let the crows croak even if they are cardinals: nobody can stop God's plan.

I really do hope that the good Montini[2] will carry on the line laid down by John: after all it is irreversible and . . . you will see what the Council will say and do!

I have spoken to Papà and he seemed better than you told me. For my part I shall do my best to be near him if it should please God. But I know nothing yet.

What is most likely is that I will accompany Father Voillaume to Rome in September-October.

For the rest we shall have to see.

However, I can tell you one thing: this period I have spent here in the Pyrenees has been really exceptional for me. God Himself wanted it and He has clasped me to Himself more closely than before.

Let us leave it to Him and everything will be peace and love.

Love,

Carlo

66

St Laurent de Neste, July 11th 1963

My dearest,

I have received official notice from Father Voillaume that he wants me in Rome with him at the end of September.

Naturally he speaks of a period and not yet of a definitive assignment to the Rome Brotherhood.

I dare not speak too much about this problem to the Lord. I prefer to tell my King and Lord Jesus that He should act according to His will for good, irrespective of any minor human feelings.

He has always guided me and I can assure you, Dolce, that every time I have had . . . surprises I have had cause to be glad of them. Yet again, therefore, 'Be it done unto me according to His sweet will.'

I have received your letter from Rapallo and I'm grateful to you for the lovely things you tell me. I have also received the magazine about the great John and I will look after it carefully.

I have begun to gather together a lot of things about him, convinced as I am that a great saint has passed through our lives.

I have written a letter to his worthy Successor and will speak to you about it when we meet.

God is guiding his Church with a special wave of grace. After all, there's so much need of it nowadays given the crisis of souls.

Tell the Mother that I shall intensify my prayers for her.

Carlo

67

Montant,[1] January 2nd 1964

My dearest Dolce,

I'm finishing my spiritual exercises in a little village near Lourdes. I have spent eight days of great peace and prayer. The day after tomorrow I go back to St Laurent where my daily duty awaits me.

How happy I am! How I feel the help of God! How I feel myself to be guided by Him! How good the Lord is!

Your letter arrived before my departure and I brought it with me. You're always so faithful! Even the famous coffee machine has arrived and so you can stop worrying about us not being able to drink coffee. Thanks for the Roman news. We really have been lucky. With Anna – despite the inevitable little difficulties – our dear old Papà will spend his last years basically happy. That's no small thing and I feel gratitude towards that woman. She has her shortcomings, but basically she is sane, good and looks after Papà so that he could not want better. After all he's happy, and this is everything.

I've also had a letter from Piero and I count on writing to my great bishop of a brother tomorrow.

You remind me about Mamma and I'm grateful to you. Great and dear Mamma! The more time passes, the more we learn to love her, to value her, to esteem her. She was a great woman. Her roots were in the Rovea family, but how much faith sprang from that little root! How much common sense. God kept it shielded from our eyes. Perhaps in order not to upset her humility he let a few little character defects appear in her at the end, but what strength there was under the shield. And what a level of prayer she reached! I feel she is already with God and I turn to her with trust and sweetness.

I haven't yet written to Lili, I haven't yet found the right tone and I'm waiting for inspiration. In any case I'll do it before returning to St Laurent.

I spent Christmas quietly with my Brothers. Afterwards I left immediately for my spiritual Exercises. I have received many graces in these blessed days and I am at great peace with God.

I refer you back to the book, which ought to come out soon. Especially the chapters on contemplative prayer and 'The Last Place'.

I have corrected a little the impression you hinted at in the chapter on poverty. It seems to me it can go ahead now.

I pray to God that 1964 will enrich you with something really new, good and beautiful.

I don't know what, but I know God is not short of ingenuity and imagination.

For my part, I would just like a little humility, but not for itself, just to fill myself more with God and pray better.

Give me a helping hand as you always do.

Love,

Carlo

68

St Laurent de Neste, March 5th 1964

Dear Dolce,

When Anna spoke to me on the telephone about needing an operation and convalescence to follow, I naturally was looking for solutions along the lines that you were thinking of.

I too think Papà would prefer to stay at home and that one of us could take Anna's place.

You ask me for the summer but *I have the feeling that it would be easier for me to ask for the months of April-May*, given that the sick Brother left for El Abiodh the day before yesterday. I don't know anything definite, and I don't know my Superiors' thoughts, but if you can give me confirmation, I will try to take it up immediately with Father Prior. Anna could undergo the operation and go to the seaside as soon as possible. It's a good season for someone who needs only to breathe the salt air, and the prices are lower.

What do you say? At any rate you should know that I *would willingly do two months of my Brotherhood life with my father*. This is a gift from Providence: to be able to live a little longer together before being separated . . . isn't it?

I look forward to hearing what you think [. . .].

Ciao dear sister. Love,

Carlo

69

St Laurent, March 21st 1964

My dearest Dolce,

As you know, I have had to put off my arrival in Italy. When my Superiors learned of Anna's operation they immediately decided that I should take her place next to Papà. But then . . . since the operation was not performed and I was useful here, they reversed the decision.

But all this says is that my Superiors are well-disposed towards me and towards Papà. Now that you know what happened, be on the look out. When you see that I can be of use in Rome, let me know.

I still don't know how the two-month plan might work out and I think you're planning an intrigue. In any case tell Papà not to worry and that his son will willingly do his Brotherhood life with him when he needs it.

Things are as usual here: peaceful. The manager of La Scuola[1] has let me know that he has to get on with reprinting the book because it is sold out in the shops.

I hurried to get it off and I'm pleased with it. I have introduced a few improvements into the second edition.

I would like to take the opportunity to wish you and Mother Angela a Holy Easter in the Lord. Greet Sister Giovanna for me as well, and tell her that when I'm in Turin I will give her an autographed copy of the book. For the time being I have no copies.

I send you a warm hug,

Carlo

70

St Laurent, June 23rd 1964

Dearest Dolce,

This will be perhaps my last letter from St Laurent de Neste.

I think I shall be leaving on Saturday evening to arrive in Rome Sunday evening (the 28th) at 10:20 pm. I shall stay in Rome at least a week before departing again for my new post in Sardinia.

Therefore you can reply to the Salesian who asked you for *the Rome address*.

The Sardinia address is as follows:

Little Brother Carlo
Monteponi near Bindua[1] (Cagliari).

After ten years I'm definitively coming back to Italy.

I'm coming back with a new message[2] for the evangelization of the poor and still more for our own sanctification.

So I'm closing one period of my life to open another.

May God grant that I should keep the peace I have come to know in these last ten years, and that it may grow.

If you telephone Papà, give him the news of my arrival on Sunday evening.

I send you a big hug,
Love,

Carlo

71

Bindua, July 6th 1964

Dearest Sister,

Here I am again on the dear old island. This time I'm further south than Bono.[1] The countryside is very hot, almost African; there's a lot of poverty. The Brotherhood lives in a squalid valley made ugly and dusty by the gashes of three mines which discharge rubbish, noise and unhappiness upon the people.

This is the right place for us just as much as Africa was, and there must be no lack of patience and courage. The people love us excessively and hold us in high regard because without the Brotherhood they would feel abandoned. Pray that I may be faithful to love and prayer. *There's a public telephone right in the village*, so sometimes I'll be able to hear your voice.

For the time being I send you a hug in Jesus.
Love,

Carlo

72

Bindua, November 29th 1964

Dearest Dolce,

I received your express letter yesterday. Thanks. As regards home, I can only give my approval. If Papà is happy to go to Lili for a few days, so much the better: it will be like a holiday. I should be passing through Rome in December immediately after Christmas. If Papà should need me, I could stay a few days with him.

As regards the financial question concerning Anna, don't argue. We've got to . . . make do. It's extremely difficult to find solutions nowadays. *We've found a good one since Papà is happy:* let's not rock the boat for the sake of a few pennies; let's leave the two of them in peace.

I've told Emerenziana that I'm paying out of my pension. With Anna I'm quick to do so even if she demands 31 thousand. *Excellent, it's still cheap*. Other than her it would cost 40,000, you can be sure.

Here things are going well and there's a lot of work. *Letters from the Desert* is in its fifth edition and comes out at Christmas with additions and an improved presentation.

Pray for me always. I've so much need.

I send you a big hug,

Carlo

73

Bindua, April 4th 1965

My dearest Dolce,

Thanks for your good wishes, which reached me along with those of Emerenziana and Piero. 55 *years old!* It's already a lot and I feel tired of living. I don't think I shall have to add many more of them. In any case I humbly accept whatever God wills. I would like to be able to fill this final period just with love, such, such love, but I feel myself so selfish, shut in, incapable and empty. Help me constantly with your prayer, in which I have always trusted.

I've begun the first chapters of a new book: *Love is for Living*[1], in which I would like to sum up the core of the gospel and biblical problem. It will not be easy, but I'm putting everything into it.

After Easter – probably from May 10th to 20th – I shall make a quick dash for Rome and who knows, perhaps Turin. I'll let you know. For the time being I send you a hug and greetings to your incomparable Mother Angela.

Love,

Carlo

74

Spello,[1] August 27th 1965

Dearest,

I know you're always complaining about your brother's silence *but I think I shall die before I learn* to change. You've got to have patience. They tell me it's a fault . . . of writers! Do you understand? In a few years I'll publish another book of *Letters* and so make up for the delays. Meanwhile *Letters from the Desert* is in its seventh edition and continues to sell. Now they've translated it in France and Venezuela.

Here at Spello we have opened a Brotherhood which – I think – will become a Novitiate or Postulancy. Anyway, on September 20th I'm going back to Bindua to spend the winter. In the new year, you watch, they'll send me here. *You're right to understand*

nothing of what my Superiors are up to: they are following God's plans . . . which are always incomprehen-
sible.

Didn't you know that?

But I'm not angry and I can assure you that I'm
greatly at peace. What is more, I always end up
understanding that it is much better to abandon ourselves
to the mysterious action of events, beneath which it is God
who is acting.

I saw Papà in Segni. I can tell you that I found him
particularly *sprightly.* That shrewd old fox Anna had
her eyes open and saw rightly that the place was
especially suited to Papà. The air, the climate, the
house: a real find. On September 15th I shall go to
Rome and spend a few days with Pierino, always
assuming both of us are still alive.

And won't you come too?

Greet my *well-beloved* France for me, with its not
overly likable but highly competent inhabitants, to
whom it behoves us Italians *to listen especially as*
regards the spiritual life and the apostolate.

Love,

Carlo

75

Bindua, December 6th 1965

My dearest,

Thanks for your warm remembrance, which I
heartily reciprocate. I would so much have liked a
quick dash to Rome before Piero's departure, but I

submitted to the sacrifice so as to become poorer. And then there's no shortage of work here and I have a sick Brother who needs help. Have patience! May God grant us another get-together on this Earth with Papà, Piero and you sisters!

The Council has certainly been a great thing! It's such a new beginning in the Church that it will force everybody to speed up. The religious Congregations – if they don't want to be left behind – will have to review many of their positions, really many, many of them, especially as regards the biblical formation of their followers. I too have seen that picture with texts taken from my writings. What can you expect . . . when you become a famous author you're quoted!!!

Things are fine here. I have two French Brothers with me and we get along together perfectly. It's wonderful. Did you see that Rome has readmitted the worker priests?![1] How many bitter pills the traditionalists have got to swallow! I really feel for them, the poor things (not the bitter pills, but the cardinals who said *it was unspeakable for a priest to work with his hands*). As though Jesus had not spent thirty years as a workman!

Thanks for the prayers, sister. I'm going through a period of great peace and interior joy. I pray for you as well.

Love,

Carlo

76

Bindua, May 30th 1966

Dearest Dolce,

I'm waiting for a telephone call and I would like to take advantage of the time to reply to your last letter, which reached me this morning.

I'm pleased about Piero's answer. You can see that . . . you women are alarmists!

And let's take the opportunity to reply to your . . . second alarm, concerning my clothes. I don't know whether you saw on television the film about *St Francis*,[1] broadcast about the beginning of May [. . .].

When they talk about poverty, it's *all theory*, but when they get down to practice they come out with excuses about cleanliness and neatness. And they end up spending and spending and doing nothing about charity. There are some Very Reverend Sisters who although they have taken a vow of poverty are dressed in the finest habits and would not set foot outside the house in old shoes.

What reigns in the world, my dear sister, is vanity, and people are afraid of being seen as fools and really poor. I on the other hand prefer to be seen as a fool, and would to God that I had a mind as truly poor as the poor who do not have a change of shirt. Remember, my sister, these three famous vows have become a mask, especially that of poverty, and the world no longer believes in the religious, and it is quite right not to. So let me go about badly-dressed and, *if anything, advise me to be poorer because my wardrobe is still full of too many things while people are dying of hunger in Africa and Asia.*

Isn't that so?

As regards cleanliness you may be right, but the subject is too long and I'll have it out with you another time.

Papà? The blame is only half his! If his ears were not continually ringing with Anna's observations, he would worry less. After all, now I'm older than fifty and close to death I can allow myself to try to die by myself without worrying about the vanity of going into it well-dressed.

Have you never read about St Philip Neri that in order to humiliate himself he used to go out with one sock or with a tear in his trousers? It's a question of seeing *whether it was he who was mad* or whether those contemporary Italians are mad who, provided they can go about well-dressed, run up debts or even don't eat!

After all, my dear sister, it is not as though we do not *accept help* from those who are good to us, but we prefer to work for things that suit the poor, rather than things that are elegant and make those we live with feel envious.

Everything else is peaceful. On June 20th I leave for Spello. Don't get angry if I don't always agree with you. I love you very, very much.

Love,

Carlo

77

Spello, July 4th 1966

My dearest and faithful Dolce,

What can I say to you? That you're good and that you pay back this rascal of a brother of yours with acts of eternal generosity. Thank you.

We'll see . . . about the generals. Supposing we were to put forward as general not a brother-in-law but the young lady [. . .]?! She'd look beautiful wearing a busby. She's got the scowl already!

Love,

Carlo

78

Spello, March 30th 1967

My dearest,

I'm making use of your present of notepaper. Thanks for the lovely gift and still more for your constant thoughtfulness.

I feel however . . . that you are *tired*. Poor Dolce! You've done some work in these nearly sixty years. But the reward is close and it will be a truly great one. In fact, as the psalm says, *'I will quench your thirst in the stream of my delights'* and it is God who is speaking.

When are you coming to spend a day in adoration here at Spello? I would be so pleased to spend a day in prayer with you before dying.

Greet the ever good Mother Angela for me and tell her that I love her and that I remember her every day to the Father.

Love,

Carlo

79

Spello, April 20th 1967

My dearest Dolce,

Thanks for the thought – I am sure it was yours – of the Moncalvo shirts.

I have written to Sister Maria to thank her, but now I am writing to you for the same purpose.

I'm pleased that you like *Love is for Living* and that you read it in peace in the evening. Don't be amazed . . . if you discover you're an egotist. That's the way it is, we're all like that. And Jesus alone is able to heal us and make us capable of gratuitous *love*.

But . . . it's a long, long, long path!

I've found a lovely place for Papà: if he comes – as I hope – he will spend two calm months close to his old son. Who knows whether you and Emerenziana might not be able to take advantage of Papà's stay in Spello to make a quick trip! It would be so lovely to spend a day in prayer together!

Love,

Carlo

80

Spello, June 9th 1967

Dearest,

Don't worry about the repayment. I'm well able to make my dear little sisters a gift out of my pension! So there's nothing to fear and I'm grateful to the Lord for giving me the opportunity to let you know that I'm your brother. All right?

Try to spend a day over here. It would be a lovely gift to me.

I don't think it will be difficult to sell the house, just put an advertisement in the newspaper and fix a fair price. You'll see that everything will go well.

I've been in the south and I've seen the Daughters of Mary Help of Christians in many places.

For the rest, everything is fine and peaceful, very peaceful!

Love,

Carlo

81

Spello, September 13th 1968

Dear Dolce,

Thank you for your lovely long letter. Thank you.

Let's hope that everything will end peaceably. It's certain that I will do my best to convince Mother Fortunée.

Don't worry about my departure for Africa. I need

it: I'm going there to pray after a period of two years rather full of activity.

You'll see that everything will turn out well.

I've been to Rome and found Papà *in particularly good form*.

I spent a lovely peaceful day with him [. . .].

My dear sister, don't overtire yourself. The time is drawing close. *You'll see that the Chapter will bring in many changes and, God willing, a little rest for you.*

I really would like you to ditch your job and be sent to a rest home *just to pray and to love*.

I really do hope for that.

Ciao.

Carlo

82

Spello, Feast of the Little Flower 1969

My dearest Dolce,

I thought of you again in Rapallo and the news of your admission to hospital confirms my suspicion that my worry about your health was not exaggerated. For the time being carry on enjoying this period of transition calmly and peacefully, trying as much as possible to give yourself over to contemplative prayer (follow in depth the six chapters on prayer in the book *In Search of the Beyond*[1] and make your own the prayer of the Russian pilgrim[2] which is very, very important for entering into the spirit of *quiet*.

Thank you for what you say about the book. I'll send you a few copies of it (one with a new dedication) and I'll send you more if they're any use to you. Would you like a parcel of twenty copies for your use? I'll let you have them immediately.

Papà is well and I hope to see him next week. I have had the Council of the Congregation here at Spello and they only left tonight. What a relief! And what work it's been, my poor sister! You know what it's like!

Pierino has written to me from his new address. I didn't know that he is president of the Commission for non-Christians: this work will be good for him because of all the contacts.

I'm going back down to Béni-Abbès on *October 20th* and I shall stay there – God willing – until Easter.

I'm beginning a new book about the *Night of Transition*[3] which I will publish in a few years' time. It is the most demanding of them all and I want to dedicate several years to it.

Pray for this, because in this book I would like to help my soul and that of my Brothers in *passing over*, which is not easy. After all, there's a little of this passing over every evening and faith is as dark as the night, but as sweet as the hand of God!

Sister Fortunée has written to me, but vaguely. She tells me that my books are selling like hot cakes in France. God be praised! This pleases me because the French are . . . *real critics*.

Don't you agree?

Write to me again before my departure. I'll try, now that you're ill, not to get myself told off.

I love you.

Love,

Carlo

83

Ventimiglia, October 8th

Dearest Sister,

As this old 'carretto' [cart][1] is about to take to the tracks of the Sahara again, I would like to send you my thanks for our last meeting in Turin. I too was moved and felt you to be close and understanding as never before. Let us learn from the death of Sister Vittorino to live every moment in love and peace until we meet her again up there in the porter's lodge of Paradise.

I send you a warm hug,

Carlo

84

Spello, October 13th 1969

Dearest Dolce,

Let us hope that your osteoporosis can indeed be relived. Thank you for what you tell me about the book and not just about the book. You really are a fine sister whom the Lord should long preserve. I will be in Rome next Friday to celebrate Papà's ninetieth. We're putting off the solemn celebrations however until Pierino's return in Spring. Then there will be all of us, God willing.

I leave for Béni-Abbès about the 25th. I have had to put it off on account of the floods in Tunisia. I'm very happy to hold off a little while: life here is so

busy! We'll write to each other often. Ciao little sister.
Courage during the sleepless nights.

Love,

Carlo

Petit Frère Carlo – Béni-Abbès (Saoura) Algeria

85

Béni-Abbès, November 17th 1969

Dear Dolce,

You are always sweet despite the fact that your
naughty brother Carlo does not write to you.

I'm at peace in the desert and the only thorn is
Papà, but . . . you'll see that God will make him wait
at least until my return. I don't deserve such grace,
but I know God is great!

Would you like to help me with your prayers in
my new labour of writing *The Night of Transition*? I'm
planning to get down to it during these months, if I
manage it.

Don't get angry with me: you know what I'm like!

And after all it's your fault. You're the Minister of
Posts and you took away from me the whole of that
charism in the bosom of my mother.

Ciao,

Carlo

86

Béni-Abbès, November 18th 1969

Dear Dolce,

Greetings from the homeland of my heart: the desert. I reached Béni after a good though long journey, to find Brother Ermete[1] waiting for me anxiously, given his loneliness.

We have now begun the life of the Brotherhood and started our work. There's building work to finish, there's people to receive and above all . . . there's prayer, which is and remains our most demanding work. I would like to take advantage of this period to make a genuine step forward in my intimacy with God: you too can help me with your prayers. I hope that everything in Italy is peaceful. I have received greetings from Emerenziana. Let's hope Papà has a good winter I saw Lili and Mario before leaving, and found them really well. Mario is making genuine progress on the road to peace and serenity. This is important.

Let us stay united in affection and . . . best wishes for your new job.

Love,

Carlo

87

Béni-Abbès, January 28th 1970

My dear Sister,

From the tone of your letter I see . . . that your old self has returned so that means your health has improved.

Thanks for the news, even if not all of it is good.

Poor old Papà, he's paying for his ninety years. He shows that we're not made for this Earth.

The plight of people on earth is so tragic!

They are really *condemned*, and if it were not for faith they would all be accursed. Dying on their feet – losing their memory – being hungry and having no food – broken down by illness!

And what a gift is the hope of heaven! The certainty that everything will have a joyful outcome!

I'm finishing my work of being in charge here at Béni-Abbès. I shall be back around Easter. I have written to Piero asking him if . . . he wants to spend a few days' retreat in the desert. You know his reply. We shall see.

Thanks for the commission from *La Stampa*.

I've let Papà have a bit of money for extra expenses. At least he won't have grumbles about that.

Well done Anna and well done Mario. They are generous. Lili has written me a lovely letter. She too is full of trust in God and it comes out in testing times. *Don't worry*. In short: I've got some fine sisters.

Ciao and pray for me.

I love you.

Carlo

88

Béni-Abbès, March 6th 1970

Dear Sister,

The time of departure is getting close. I wanted to spend Lent here in order to have peace for prayer. I'm so happy even if this time the desert has been especially harsh. Perhaps it is a preparation for my next book, the very subject of which will be the difficulty of faith, *The Night of Transition*.

I see that Papà is being brave and hanging on. I have the feeling that the Lord will give us the joy of one more almost plenary meeting of the 'carretti' [little carts] . . . As regards Piero: he's not coming here. We are to meet at *Spello*. The affair of the meeting with the Buddhists caused him to delay his coming and the plan to make the return journey together has gone up in smoke. Patience!

Would you have the kindness to send the enclosed postcard to Mother Fortunée? I don't have her address.

Thank you. Courage, Dolce. God is the greatest.

(Carlo)

89

Béni-Abbès, December 3rd 1970

Dear Dolce,

I'm sorry to have hurt you. But I had written to Piero telling him to come in Spring on the occasion of his journey with the Buddhists. I had also written to you . . . You are the Minister of Posts and Post-cards and know how to put up sales of postage stamps. I on the other hand only write about things *I feel* and are *new*. I don't know how to repeat well-worn sentences. Have patience. If you only knew the number of letters I put in the waste-paper basket! I receive heaps of letters from men and women who read my books and if I were to write to them all I would spend at least ten hours a day. Do you see?

Coming back to ourselves: I'm asking the Lord for the grace to see Papà once more on this Earth. But . . . his will be done!

Things are going well here. I'm working hard on my new book which is costing me a lot. You too, pray for us because it isn't easy to say the things I feel inside.

I can't tell you to stay close to Papà because you're doing it, but . . . given my absence you've got to take my place.

I've had a letter from Emerenziana. She . . . is kinder than you and never tells me off about my silences. She pretends to understand!!!

Ciao Dolce, wish me well even if I write few post-cards.

However, you see that every now and then I write you a book and this should count for a little. Shouldn't it? Ciao.

Love,

Carlo

90

Béni-Abbès, December 15th 1970

Dearest Dolce and Emerenziana,

I'm writing to you in the tent where I'm staying a few miles from the Brotherhood, right out in the desert.

I've come here to do a period of retreat in preparation for Christmas.

It's a harsh but very beautiful life: stars and cold by night, Stone Age cooking, strong sun by day. The chapel is a little cave hollowed out of the steep side of an ancient volcano.

I'm trying to be converted, but it isn't easy at the age of sixty. My skin has become hard and dry and my heart drier still. I think about you, about Papà, about Piero, about Mamma, about the living, about the dead, about all peoples.

I carry you with me in prayer. I shall stay here another week, then return to Béni-Abbès where Brother Ermete is waiting for me.

I haven't much news but I expect some on my return for Christmas.

Within a month the Novices will arrive here and then Father Voillaume, who is just coming to preach their retreat.

As regards Papà, I'm pleased he has picked up. He has written to me telling me not to worry because he is not yet 'moribund'.

I'm trying to get on with my new book but . . . What labour! I'm as dry as the sand!

I don't know yet if I'll make it. Pray for me, my

dear sisters. We'll see if Piero will come here in Spring!

At any rate, my bishop from Foligno[1] will come. I invited him and he has accepted.

Have you read my article about deacons? It came out in the Assisi *Rocca*.[2] Read it.

A big hug tinged with sand and smoke and other desert things.

Love,

                                             Carlo

91

                              Béni-Abbès, Epiphany 1971

Dear Dolce,

I really wasn't expecting this gift for Epiphany!

To learn that you are in bed with a leg in traction, to learn that you have been the victim of an attack, is certainly no pleasure. You see, you see what becomes of elegant, well-dressed Sisters with handbags under their arms!

I've always upheld the thesis that one should dress badly, in torn habits, carrying ragged bags!!! Thieves are less inclined to attack the poor.

And the beauty of it is that you too were poor because you had nothing on you . . . but you see, you looked like an elegant lady, a sort of chief executive with a full handbag.

Poor Dolce, you had to go through this too!

Now what advice can be given to a bedbound Sister, what can be said to comfort her a little? Here you are, it can be said that it's not all black, that to stay still in bed for forty days can be lucky. A good retreat, a high-class Lent, an opportunity to read the whole Bible . . . in short a real piece of good luck.

There's nothing else to be said!

Naturally your Inspector will not be of the same opinion, but overall things will settle down and you'll see that the world will carry on just the same.

However, one thing: I'd like to ask you for a . . . rosary every day for my new book which is getting on fairly well but needs lots and lots of light from above.

It's a pity you're not in the same room as Papà, in Rome!

I'm rushing to catch the post because it's leaving and I send you a hug, even though you've got a leg less.

Love,

Carlo

92

Béni-Abbès, January 20th 1971

Dear 'mugged' sister,

I would never have thought that a sweet little thing like you could become the target of wicked men!

How's your little wheel doing now? Don't you feel closer to your brother with his flat tyre?

Don't worry! You'll see that, like me, one day you'll say: *'It was a real grace from the Lord.'*

It's always like that for those who love God: *Everything is grace!*

Are you praying for my book?
How dry the way is!
I've got as far as a third of the labour.

I receive regular news from Papà and the friends who stop by to visit him. I really do hope to have the joy of embracing him again and being with him once more. And afterwards . . . with you. We go ahead with courage. Ciao. I send you a very warm hug.

Carlo

93

B.A. February 24th 1971

Dear Dolce,

Happy Lent! Your long letter reached me yesterday. Thank you.

Don't worry about defending the book. It's the Salesians who ought to worry about forgetting prayer on the excuse of sociology! What about the title? It's good to create a scandal if it provokes meditation on the truth. *In Search of the Beyond* has a good ring and is getting truer and truer.

Keep on praying for the *new* one which should be more complete.

I'll be going back to Rome immediately after Easter and I'll stay a few days with Papà. I'm really well and greatly at peace.

Love,

Carlo

94

Béni-Abbès, March 20th 1971

Dear Dolce,

Thanks for your long letter and alleluia that you are better. I'll see you soon.

I return to Italy via Tunis-Naples on April 20th. *I'll go straight to Rome and I'll stay a few days with Papà. I need to do that.* There is no hurry to return to Spello [. . .].

On the 24th I'll have to be in France for the Council and either on the way or on my return I hope to see you at Turin.

I'm longing to give you a hug! My book . . . is really going as *I wanted: driven on . . . by Him, the Holy Spirit. You will be pleased.*

On the arrival of Piero . . . a new rally of the 'carretti' . . . Will it be the last? Ciao. Pass on this news to Emerenziana.

Carlo

95

Béni-Abbès, March 24th 1971

Dear Dolce,

I am leaving by car straight after Easter and since I'm disembarking at *Marseilles* I hope to pass by Turin.

I'm counting on being *with you at 11.00 on Thursday April 9th.*

I hope to find you there. I'll go directly to 14 via Cumiana.

Goodbye then and I'm really looking forward to seeing you.

Love,

Carlo

96

Spello, May 18th 1971

Dear Dolce,

This time our meeting will present difficulties. Be patient. I'll be in Rome on the 28th and leave for Naples on the afternoon of the 29th. From Naples I fly to Milan on the morning of the 30th.

It won't be possible to go to *Moncalvo* this time. I'll be in Turin on Thursday 3rd for the evening conference. It won't be difficult for your fellow sisters to find the conference site, all the more so since it's a small town.

At any rate, the organizer is Fr G. Barra,[1] Adult Vocations Seminary, Turin.

I'm pleased that you'll be staying a while with Papà. Don't squabble with Anna. She's not in a position to understand you. Let her be. What matters is that Papà should be happy and he is so. The rest . . . will sort itself out in time. Anna has a thousand shortcomings but she has the *unique quality of understanding Papà and really helping him with her presence and her care*. This is what matters. I'll write to tell

Emerenziana to make available to Papà *a good portion of her summer*.

Papà is at the end and it is up to us, his children, to be as close to him as possible. I'll do my part too.

I think that when Piero arrives we will be able to get together towards the middle of June. What do you think?

Things are good here. My Superiors have understood that Spello is important. It's taken five years, but they've got there.

The Lord gives us sweets but also . . . a hard look through our brothers.

Isn't that so?

During the days I spent in France I saw as never before the action of God in my life.

It's a really lovely thing!

Love,

Carlo

97

Spello, 21st August 1971

Dear Dolce,

Lili and Mario left again yesterday for Rome after spending a week here. They are at peace. I'm pulling my "carretto" [little cart] as best I can. I really yearn for the desert this time and I'm counting off the days. It has been a burdensome year. The Lord gives me strength but now I need to be silent.

I'll leave on October 8th.

I feel that you too are noticing the weight of the journey.

We've got to cut down on activity and increase our contemplation, otherwise we'll be in trouble.

Thanks for the shirts. I'll write to Sister Maria Casaro.

I was in Isola for a conference and lunched with Anna. She's low, but still holding her own. She was at ease and pleased with the visit.

Ciao: keep your courage up and pray for me.

Carlo

98

Spello, February 8th 1972

Dear Dolce,

I finally succeeded in finding the number of the Review dedicated to Our Lady and I'm sending it to you in a collection I count on having back . . . When you've finished.

Thanks!

Lili and Mario were here recently and I enjoyed their company. This evening I leave for France where the Council of the Congregation will be held. I shall return on the 17th, ready to leave again for Puglia, where I shall stay until February 28th.

As you can see, I'm spending almost the whole of February outside the Brotherhood. In March I shall go to the Veneto, in April to Emilia-Romagna, in *May to Piedmont*. In this way I satisfy all the requests for lectures which I had building up.

My health is good and I'm getting by.

From time to time the temptation comes upon me (but it could be that it's not a temptation) to take to the desert again and spend the last years of my life there. What do you think?

I see that Piero has finally received the books.

Dear sister. May God bless you with his Love.

Love,

Carlo

99

Spello, March 5th 1972

Dear Dolce,

Tell your fellow sister that it is not possible for the time being. However, I will take on the commitment during my return from Africa, since I have to pass through Spain, more or less in the *summer of 1973*.

They've also invited me to Venezuela. Poor me!

And to think that my only other possibility coming up is to go to Paradise.

I yearn for it because I'm tired and incapable.

Pray for me, sister.

I shall be in Piedmont the 17th–18th–19th May.

Carlo

100

Béni-Abbès, February 1st 1973

Dearest Dolce,

What a lovely letter you've written me! Well done. I see you're beginning to make progress!

As regards the reviews you tell me about, bear in mind that I am isolated here. I have read nothing and would be grateful if you will send them to me.

I'll write to Piero. The foreign editions are doing well. The English one, published in New York, has been particularly successful. I'll spend the months of February and March doing more writing. At the beginning of April I leave for Spello, where I'll be for Holy Week.

My health is good but – as you say – tiredness is beginning to set in. The last stages are the hardest but before us we have the teaching of Jesus' Cross.

Ciao. God bless you.

Carlo

101

Spello, Pentecost 1974

Dear Sisters,

I'm sending you this document[1] written by my Congregation to the Bishops.

For his part, Father Voillaume has written the same things to the Pope.

Believe me, if you still have any trust, the Bishops'

order about the Referendum was *not binding on con-
science. If there had been a single doubt, do you think that
I would have set myself in disagreement with the Church?
Thirty years ago the same thing happened to me with Pius
XII.*

Time has proved me right.

But you, like so many immature Christians, have
only a great fear of the Church and instead of working things out you stay on the surface. Be patient!
You will understand in time.

Carlo

102

Spello, June 1974

Dearest Sisters and dear Piero,

If there is one thing for which we ought to thank the
Lord, it is that of being born into a genuine Christian
community. When I think of Papà and Mamma and
what they did to bring us up in the faith, I end up
lost for words with which to say thank you to the
Lord for the gifts showered upon us.

We were poor and we were happy. We were from
an obscure suburban family and we loved one
another so well that we did not dare ask anything
from God unless the grace to praise him for ever.

Do you remember when we used to go to the
parish church of Saint Egidio in Moncalieri or the
Salesian chapel on the Via Piazzi in Turin to say the
rosary during May? All of us were there and our

family was enough to fill those little old churches with prayer.

Then we grew up and began to leave home.

You were the first, Piero, leaving for the missions as a Salesian. I remember your eyes, on fire with zeal. That was life! And when later I saw your little missionary's room under the great coconut palms of Bang-Nok-Kuek, I understood for the first time the poverty of a real missionary, risking everything, heat, tropical diseases and tiredness, in the cause of the Gospel of Jesus.

Then you left, Emerenziana, to become a nun with the Daughters of Mary Help of Christians. For me your departure was more painful than that of Piero.

I missed you a lot just as a sister, and it was then that I understood how demanding Jesus is to require of us such painful separations for His kingdom.

But the suffering was not over, because two years later you, Dolcidia, told me that you too wanted to consecrate yourself to God.

I didn't tell many people about my hurt, but I still remember the tears I used to hide in the sheets of my bed. I hadn't yet understood the demands of God's love, and to see the house emptied of you sisters, of whom I was so fond, caused me suffering which I did not easily forget.

Meanwhile the years passed and . . . and my turn came.

With me God used a different tactic. First he demanded my activity, then he demanded me. I lived through two distinct periods and both of them were very beautiful. In the first I found myself working in the Church like a crusader; I felt myself worth something, and I threw myself into activity with the zeal of a lover.

My love was the Church.

They were years of genuine commitment. My life sailed down a river of love and community life: meetings, gatherings, speeches. I even had the feeling of 'making it', and in my naiveté I found myself praying like this: 'Lord, let us get on with it, you'll see that we'll bring everybody to your feet as King of the universe.'

But he who always puts up with our immaturity was lying in wait for me. I heard myself told by him: 'Carlo, I don't want your activity any more, I want you.'

And I found myself in the desert as though it were a second period of my life, to empty myself of my securities and free myself from idols. It has been the most splendid adventure of my life, even if it has been the roughest and most painful.

Things can be seen more clearly from the desert and in a more eternal perspective. The cosmos takes the place of your country of birth and God becomes a real absolute. Even the Church takes on the wider dimensions of the universe and 'those far away', that is those who are not yet visibly Christians, become neighbours.

I ended up on Islamic soil just as you, Piero, had meanwhile become bishop in a Buddhist country.

The first lesson you learn when you love non-Christians is tolerance. Little by little your arrogant wish to lay down the law to others fades away and you end up feeling yourself a poor exile in a foreign land. There's another thing you learn from those who don't share your faith: that God is their God and isn't waiting for you in order to reach them with his spirit which is love.

In this way the boundaries of the Church are infinitely extended and you live in the comfort of thinking how Jesus died for all and has already touched all with his supreme sacrifice.

The time will come when they too will join the visible Church, but potentially they are already there, and you ought to adopt an attitude of great respect and love towards them.

And above all you must not judge them, as Jesus taught us.

These things came back into my thoughts just recently when, without wanting to, I found myself in the whirlwind of the referendum.

I know that I have scandalized you and this is why it was right that I should write to explain myself to you whom I love.

My God! How awful is the thought of causing suffering to those you love! What agony I had at the time! Thinking that I was a cause of division for thousands of my brothers and sisters with whom I had prayed in liturgical assemblies and with whom I had broken the Bread of life, has been an intolerable hurt.

But it was the truth that upheld me and 'set me free' even in the jaws of death and frightful contradictions.

And what is this truth?

It is the truth which blossomed and flowered from the root of my vocation as a Little Brother and yours, dear Piero, as a bishop among the Buddhists of Thailand. It is the truth of tolerance.

It is the truth that in the post Conciliar Church

something radically different has been introduced into our history.

Buddhist for you, and Islam for me, have taught us to live in a foreign country no longer as masters but as exiles, and to understand in depth those who do not yet share our own faith.

But you will tell me: here we're in Italy. Yes, we're in Italy, but is Italy still Christendom? No. *This is one of the most obvious signs of the times which we ought to grasp: Italy is a jumble* of ideologies, a mission country, a land where Christians (not by baptism, but by faith) are becoming a minority.

So this is the real problem posed by the divorce referendum: is it the indissolubility of marriage that is in question, or respect for those who do not share the faith?

In conscience I have no doubts in this regard.

None of us Christians can cast doubt on Jesus' own words: 'What God has joined together let no one put asunder,' but these words cannot be used as a civil law for those who do not believe in Christ's resurrection and belong to a secular society.

I am well aware that indissolubility is the perfection of marriage and the truest proposal that Christians can put before non-Christians, but can I impose it with a law on those who – much more so than our fathers – have a 'stiff neck'? *Consience had to answer this question; some answered yes, others answered no. I think that both are in the Church and had the right to express themselves.*

Our pastors' directives were a guide but were not binding in conscience.

It's useless for us who know each other to affirm our love for the Church: I think that all five of us are willing to die for it and we have given witness to that.

I'd like to end this letter of mine by supporting my case with an example which touches us close to home, even though the example only concerns the merciful manner in which the church deals with those who have fallen short, while the indissolubility of marriage is something else.

You know how the Church is suffering at this time because of those who are leaving the priesthood or the religious life. It's a phenomenon on an awful scale which involves tens of thousands of priests and Sisters.

Well then, what is the post-Conciliar Church doing? Whereas at one time it left defrocked priests excommunicated in a corner without the comfort of the sacraments until on the point of death, it has now as it were understood the Gospel more profoundly, even realizing that it was mistaken, and it opens its arms to them, readmits them to communion and gives them hope. And the same thing happens to the thousands of Sisters who have abandoned their vows. Mercy takes the place of justice and the Church shows itself to be a force for freedom to those who have fallen outside the law.

Can you feel that there's something new in the air? The Gospel is knocking as never before at the doors of a world racked by violence, disorder and sin. As Christians we have to present ourselves as the bearers, not of a religion crippled by time and our sins, but of the breath of a Gospel which is love, mercy and newness. Listen to the words of Pope John on his deathbed: 'Now more than ever, and certainly more than in centuries gone by, we are committed to serving humanity as such and not just Catholics; to defending first of all and everywhere the rights of the human person and not just those of the Catholic Church. It's not that the Gospel is changing, but we are beginning to understand it better.'

I'd like to leave you with these words and tell you of all the love which binds me to you.

Love,

Carlo

103

Spello, June 18th 1974

Dearest Dolce,

Thank you for your letter which reached me this morning. I feel you are finally more at peace.

I enclose a magazine[1] you ought to read: it contains the Brothers' documents and a discussion carried on by *real Catholics* (even the director of *Civiltà Cattolica* is included). Now they're beginning to show their cards. Believe me, Dolce: the mistake was to give the weight of an order to a simple guideline from the Bishops [. . .].

But believe me it was a mistake and it was serious. The Church comes out of this trial injured by the superficial ease of giving commands without any deep self questioning. Because I too am the Church, you are the Church.

Love,

Carlo

104

Spello, Feast of St Peter 1974

Dear Dolce,

Be at peace, as I am. The time will come when you will understand the battle I have had to fight. It has cost me, treading on my dignity and being taken for disobedient when I wasn't and I'm not.

It takes patience.

Read what Father Voillaume says.[1] Ciao.

Love,

Carlo

105

Spello, December 2nd 1974

Dear Dolce,

But is it possible that I never get anything right with you any more!!!

I'm sorry to have made you suffer again over the affair of the married clergy. I only said what some of the African bishops said at the October Synod. *Where there are no more priests do you prefer no longer to receive the Eucharist* or to accept that the Church should ordain married men? I would willingly have received Communion from Papà. But aren't you aware that you are a slave to fantasies!!! Wasn't St Peter married? I can understand that a celibate priest is better, and *in fact I have chosen celibacy*, but I would not be scandal-

ized to see the father of a family celebrating the
Eucharist.

Besides, if you live a few years longer – less than
five – you'll see it in practice in the Church.

But why should we get angry about things which
don't matter? Poor Dolce! I'm sorry to see you like
this. I wish that when you considered the faith you
referred more to apostolic times than to the pontificate of Pius XII.

I love you.

Now I'm in silence here in the hermitage. I'm
working on my new book, *Summoned by Love*[1].

I know you don't trust me any more, but I'm telling
you all the same: pray for this new book of mine.

It's all about confidence in God. I hope you'll like
it.

Love,

Carlo

106

Spello, January 22nd 1975

Dear Dolce,

You are indeed on the Pope's side, and you do
right to say so. *But what makes you think that I'm not?*[1]

The problem is this. I can be on the Pope's side
even if I disagree with him about things not concerning the faith. *I was on Pope Pius XII's side, but I had
the courage to tell him that the Latin Mass had to be
changed; that Franco was not treating the workers well in*

Spain; that the seminaries needed changing etc., etc. This is what I mean when I talk about fanaticism.

I can have different ideas from my Bishop about things which concern the civil law and the *Referendum law was a civil, not a religious law.*

Nobody can convince me that to be tolerant of an atheist is to be against the Gospel. *I tolerate the divorce* of a non-believer, I do not desire it.

Look out the current edition of *Servitium*.[2] *It's the Carmelites' magazine.* It's all about the papacy. Read it calmly and you'll see where the problem is. Fanatic means being unwilling to seek out the truth but considering yourself already the possessor of truth without thinking it through.

Everybody can say silly things, even the Bishops, and we should make sure that our obedience is an informed obedience.

Do you know what Cardinal Newman said?[3] 'I will never obey an order which is against my conscience.' Read the Gospel. How many times does Jesus disobey the Temple? Was He disobedient or was it the Temple which was no longer in the right?

It's all a mess, you see, and it was brought about by one single mistake: *The Bishops couldn't order what they ordered; they could only advise.*

Can you understand it? I love you and don't worry.

Carlo

107

Spello, February 1975

Dear Dolce,

When suffering is lived through with love it does not go to waste.

You'll see that everything that has happened will help us to become more aware and more authentic.

Ciao.

Carlo

108

Spello, July 10th 1975

Dearest Dolce,

I'm just back from a meditation given to a hundred Sisters who came to invade the Spello cloister.

I find *your* letter waiting, and since I'm in a gentle mood after the presence of so much womanly holiness, I'm replying immediately.

What can I tell you? I'm happy and at peace. The hermitages are full, people are at prayer. I have Brothers who help me, I have a house full of marvellous creatures who praise the Lord with me each evening during the great liturgy.

You'll see when you come with Piero, Lili and Emerenziana. I really hope that the Lord will grant us this grace of praying together in the same chapel before dying. I look forward very much to this visit.

I've received good reviews of my book. I've sent it

to all the Bishops. Did you say your head is empty? It's the suffering of aridity, but it always leaves some benefit in the spirit. At such times try to love a lot.

At Spello everything is booked up until next year: imagine!

Love,

Carlo

109

Spello, October 10th 1977

My dearest sisters,

Thank you for your letter which reached me this morning.

It was a lovely gift for you to live together in Roppolo this autumn. *I would willingly have made a third*! All the more so since a quiet place like that would have helped me. I'm writing my *tenth* and last book.[1] It will be called *The Desert in the City* and I reckon on getting it out by Easter.

I am especially well and feel on top form. In November I will go to some peaceful little spots with Liliana and Mario.

Here at Spello there's peace. Now the Bishops are beginning to arrive. Three of them came this week. The feeling is that the pontificate is at a turning point. These times are not easy but they're full of the Gospel. I'm so happy to live in God and let myself be carried along by him even in the littlest things!

The weather is good here and I think of your floods in Piedmont. What with the earthquake in Friuli and the floods in Piedmont and Lombardy, it might be said that the north has a few little debts to settle.

I'm really pleased that you, Dolcidia, have had the happiness of a healthy break at Roppolo. You have some really sensitive Superiors who give orders from the heart. There are some human touches which are a joy to receive. In this the Congregations are maturing a lot.

Isn't that right?

There's some movement in the Italian Church, and let's wish it well. I think the times of excommunications and harshness are over. Since I can't come with you, I send you a big hug.

Carlo

110

Béni-Abbès, 2.4.1910–2.4.1978

Dearest Dolce and Emerenziana,

As you can see, even if it's not my fault, I'm 68 years old.

I'm happy to say thank you to the Lord here in this desert which has played such a part in my spiritual life and which I am seeing – I think – for the last time.

I've made a forty day retreat and it was very beautiful.

I'm going back to Italy at the end of the month and I hope to see my tenth-born son: *The Desert in the City*. You'll see that you'll like it!

I've seen lots of friends again here, including the

Bishop[1] who ordained me deacon in this very place. Pray for this old 'Carretto' [little cart] . . . now arrived at its final oasis.

Carlo

111

Spello, June 25th 1983

My dearest Dolce,

How good you are to me!

You're right to want something in writing from me but I always excuse myself to those who are waiting by saying *that my letters are in my books*. And there are plenty of them, perhaps too many. But you are a special case, nothing less than the Carretto Minister of Posts, and so I should give you consideration outside the books, that is in letters and postcards!! Now I'll try. We had a special celebration for the twenty-fifth anniversary of Mario and Lili. Mario was magnificent and wanted to invite all the plain, poor people of the valley. What came of it was something delicious marked by the goodness which is characteristic of Mario and Lili.

I'm spending this year here and I can assure you that I'm not alone. But I'm pleased that the Lord is giving me so many comforts. If I write another book it will be about martyrdom. I feel the need for it and I think it would be good to talk about the love which overcomes pain and unites us to the Cross of Jesus. The great problem, is *to suffer with love* and nowadays, when pain is so widespread, we need to help ourselves by throwing our pain into the flames of love. What do you say about that? The book is going well. Indeed, speaking of books and cassettes, I'm sending you some stuff. It will come in useful as gifts for your friends.

The book deals with the question of marriage and the conferring of the priesthood upon married men as well.[1] It seems a big problem, but it isn't. We mustn't be frightened: the world is swinging that way and you'll see that in a little while, starting with Brazil and Africa, it will be necessary to ordain married men.

Don't be afraid, sister, and bear it in mind that your brother Carlo's vocation has always been a prophetic one. Unfortunately . . . ; because *it costs*. I love you.

Carlo

Enclosures

Rome, October 2nd 1963

To Mgr
Loris F. Capovilla
Rome

Dear Monsignor,

The writer is the former Professor Carretto, president of the GIAC, currently a Little Brother of Jesus of Father de Foucauld. I returned some time ago from the Sahara to found a Brotherhood for the sick near Lourdes, but I shall be spending this month of October here in Rome, where I have accompanied my Superior, Father Voillaume.

But let me come to my reason for writing.

I followed the pontificate of John XXIII day by day with prayers and with the distinct impression of being faced by a Pope of unique stature, and moreover one especially loved by God.

When he fell ill, I offered my life for his return to health, but I very quickly understood that God wished to pluck that altogether exceptional fruit at the exact moment of a ripeness which was to breathe a scent of Heaven to the furthest ends of the Earth.

When he died I was in France, and what happened in that country, which even though it is a secular state had understood the spirit of the deceased great man so well, was so exceptional as to convince the majority that a saint had died.

I have loved no man on Earth as I loved John XXIII, because at prayer the Lord made me feel that He was resolving the real problems which had assailed my life as a Christian. Everything is due to Him, and even over this second Session, so well begun by Paul VI, that giant's mind and spirit can be felt hovering.

Monsignor, I do not wish to trouble you further, but you might grant me a gift. I feel that you loved Pope John a lot and that you too suffered for Him.

I would very much like to hear you speak about Him. Grant me a brief audience, or better still, if you can, come to dinner one evening here in the Brotherhood. You will also meet Father Voillaume, the Prior of the Little Brothers.

As you choose, Monsignor.

In the hope of being able to meet you again, I would like to express all my gratitude for what you have done over the years for *Him*.

Your Little Brother,

Carlo Carretto

2   THE START OF THE SPELLO BROTHERHOOD

The Bishop of Foligno

Dear Bishop,

I have great pleasure in informing you that on August 15th the Little Brothers of Jesus will be coming to the Diocese.

At the moment they are fifteen postulants, who will come to the old monastery of St Jerome at Spello under the leadership of Brother Carlo Carretto.

For the time being it is an experimental stay, in the expectation that once the work on the monastery has been carried out, the Little Brothers will be able to set up in the Diocese their only house on the Italian mainland.

We are committed to the restoration work on the Monastery and the furnishing of the house.

For the furnishing I have already collected some furniture and other useful things which certain families have donated. It's a question of things which are not made use of in their homes, but which are very useful to the Little Brothers.

For the restoration, on the other hand, since we will have to face substantial expense, I have thought of asking for donations from friends of the Little Brothers, and also from people who are able to understand the importance of an Institution which is arousing so much interest in the world.

The donations can be sent directly to me or to my Secretary or also to Leonello Radi whom I have asked to coordinate the many aspects of the preparation of a poor but decent dwelling for the Little Brothers.

Confident that you will heed my request, I thank you and offer you a blessing.

Foligno, July 24th 1965

Siro Silvestri

3

While the bishop of Foligno appealed to the Local Church for practical aid for the Little Brothers, Carlo in this letter suggested to his friend Dr Leonello Radi the 'norms' for the installation of the Brotherhood.

Bindua, July 1st 1965

My very dear Leonello,

I think that these days your house is becoming a branch office of the Brotherhood.

In the great Father de Foucauld's ideal you have found a new family, and in you we have found a true brother. It is God who guides things and from all time he had already fixed these things. Is it not so?

I see that events are rushing on and exceeding all our expectations.

I would never have believed in . . . the establishment of the Spello Brotherhood in the summer of 1965!

And here it is.

So Brother Paul wants to set up an experimental postulancy from August 15th to September 15th. The idea is an interesting one, with the aim of having some Brothers in the little monastery both to give a hand with the work and to experience the new Brotherhood possibilities for life and work.

I'll be there for the whole month and probably a few days beforehand as well. This is how things stand:

1) I think that by August 15th a group of ten postulants will be there. With them we will have Manu (a Frenchman) and myself. In addition, Paolo will come for the final days.

2) It's a question of getting the . . . campsite ready for fifteen people. Paolo will have spoken to you about this. We could begin with the essentials, choosing the most suitable places that were easiest to furnish for fifteen chaps (a common dormitory, a

kitchen, a place of prayer). It doesn't matter whether they are the definitive sites. For the time being the chapel could very well be the choir of the church. Then with the Brothers on the spot we could see better how the work should develop.

3) You don't need to spend anything on materials. The Little Brothers prefer the old and used, in general what is lying in the attics and cellars of our friends. It's enough to make a list of friends and get together a list of ordinary objects: plates, glasses, mattresses, tables – a lot of tables – stools, spoons, cooking pots etc . . . etc. At the very end a lorry comes along and the house is amply furnished without spending a thing. For the beds I would say that all that is necessary is fifteen little horsehair mattresses to go on the ground on wooden planks. So cross beds off!

Wooden planks will be very useful; many things can be made out of them on the spot as well as joinery in general.

4) Many of the arrivals will be working inside the monastery and a few of them – if possible – will be able to work outside, but in the space of one month it will not be easy.

When I write to the postulants I will tell them to bring overalls with them and, should they possess one, a bicycle.

You will soon have the opportunity to see Brother John, a Frenchman who is coming to do his spiritual exercises in Umbria. Greet him for me and tell him that this morning the AMMI Mineworks has taken him on and he begins work on July 20th.

I look forward to your news. You certainly got into trouble when your path crossed that of the Little Brothers!!!

A fond greeting to your brothers, your sister, your mamma, His Lordship (how pleased he will be!), and to all our friends.

May God bless you with the strength of his immense love.

Love, Carlo

P.S. Let me know if you need money. I don't want to leave you alone in a jam, you know!

Things went as described by Carlo: the Regional Superior Paul Cheval sent two Little Brothers, Paul Collet and Emmanuel; (Manu) Brun to Spello to welcome some young men interested in a vocation to the Brotherhood.

The town council handed over to the Little Brothers of the Gospel an old Franciscan monastery dedicated to St Jerome, next to the town cemetery. Furniture and household goods came in from nearby families and religious communities, who responded in this way to the invitation both of the Bishop of Foligno and the parish priest of Spello.

4 INTERVENTIONS ON THE QUESTION OF DIVORCE

Brothers in Christ
Pastors of the Church in Italy,

May we, the Little Brothers in Italy, be allowed to come before you as sons at a time when an intervention by our Brother Carlo Caretto on the subject of the referendum has caused perplexity and misunderstanding in some minds.

Our vocation would rather incline us to silence, but on this occasion it seemed to us that such silence could be interpreted as a flight from church responsibility. Too many voices were raised around us demanding clarification on the level of conscience in the face of such a confused situation, especially on a religious level.

We do not claim that by writing his intervention Brother Carlo expressed himself in the only way possible, but it certainly represented a cry which came from the depths.

Perhaps it will have appeared inopportune and almost scandalous to many people and it is for this reason that we would like to explain the meaning of this cry and why we approve of what he was trying to say.

We felt that consciences were more disturbed and confused about the very purpose and content of the referendum.

Sometimes the impression was given of wanting to put God's word to the vote.

How could it be forgotten that Christ always wanted his words to remain a challenge without the support of external forces and prestige?

Many Christians were altogether convinced that they were rendering the church a service by voting in a certain way, often encouraged by their own Pastors.

Can this be?

And there is a reality which springs from our very ecumenical vocation as Little Brothers and from the values we saw with joy expressed by the Council: a profound respect for non-Christian minorities and for those who have lost the faith or are seeking it.

It is starting from our daily lives and from the Gospel that we feel that we must take our inspiration only from Christ, who had a preference for tax-collectors, sinners and prostitutes.

When it came to the choice, it was of them that we thought.

We are far from wishing to give lessons and we are not theologians, but it is the word of God which has guided us in our choices. Christ brought us that freedom which springs from love, following the example of him who gave himself for us even unto death, death on a cross.

This means that what saves us is no longer the law but love. 'Love is the fulfilment of the law' (Romans 13:10). We are put in mind of the heartfelt words of Paul to the Galatians when they still put a great deal of trust in certain laws: 'You make me feel I have wasted my time with you' (Galatians 4:11); 'If the Law can justify us, there is no point in the death of Christ' (Galatians 2:21).

What a great deal of concern for the law we have heard recently! Our only hope is in love. Modern society has reached such a point that only the proclamation and witness of love are still of any use to help people on their journey.

Let us no longer defend gospel values with the law.

We do not need to tell you that none of us is in favour of divorce. We are well aware how much harm it can cause. Similarly, none of us wishes to oppose that authority as pastors of the faith which comes to you from Christ.

But it has been impossible for us to understand the harshness and intransigence of some of you towards those people who were not in full agreement with your line of thought.

We could have understood it if there had been doubts within the Italian church about the indisolubility of marriage.

How can your authority as Pastors be used to oblige believers to vote for or against a civil law?

If our Church is to be a place of freedom, pluralism and tolerance, your authority can only grow.

We are spontaneously reminded of the disagreements in the early church of which the Acts of the Apostles tell us. Writing to the Galatians, Paul, dares to say: 'When Cephas came to Antioch, however, I opposed him to his face, since he was manifestly in the wrong' (Galatians 2:11).

It would be a real scandal if it were no longer possible to speak out in freedom of conscience just ten years after the Council.

In conclusion, we would like to express the difficulty which the Christian people sometimes feels when faced with the decisions of the Magisterium in such circumstances.

We feel ourselves inadequate to give a reply, but we trust in your pastoral care and in the Spirit who enlightens the Church.

Undergoing this trial will no doubt have the benefit of informing consciences still more to give witness to the gospel values within the sphere of the Church community.

May the Spirit grant us to see a new Pentecost: 'But the Advocate, the Holy Spirit, whom the Father will send in my name, will teach you everything and remind you of all I have said to you' (John 14:26).

There follow the signatures of the Regional Superior for

Europe of the Little Brothers and of the Little Brothers of the Gospel in Italy.

Rome, Vigil of Pentecost 1974

5 FATHER VOILLAUME'S LETTER

Dear Parish Priest,

I would not like to leave your letter of last May 14th unanswered, even though I think it takes great prudence to judge from France attitudes which concern the political and Church situation in Italy, both of which are very different from those we know in France.

On the other hand, I believe we must have trust in the conscience of others and therefore, even as a Superior, I would never allow myself to pass judgement on decisions taken by one of my fellow Brothers, especially when I know his honesty and genuine feeling for the church and religious values.

My hope is that we Christians will reach the point among ourselves of feeling sufficiently brothers in the faith as to respect one another even when our opinions are divergent in matters which do not touch the faith and do not cast suspicion upon loyalty to the Church in that which concerns her divine mission; but since you put the question, I would like to tell you in all honesty that the way in which the question of the retention or abrogation of a State law permitting civil divorce in certain cases and not without the fulfilment of a given number of conditions, seems to me, seen from here, to have been very ambiguous.

It is not a matter, either for Brother Carlo, or for any of us, or for the majority of Christians who voted 'NO' of bringing into question the law promulgated by Christ about the indissolubility of marriage. It was not a matter of this, but, as citizens of a country which has become pluralist, of asking whether, out of respect for those who honestly profess other doctrines, it was or was not any longer just and opportune that a law passed for all citizens, and not just Christians, should give them the possibility of civil divorce. It seems to me that such a question could in conscience be answered in different ways. I do not think that to a question posed like this the Church could impose in conscience a single reply, not even on Christians. By doing so it ran the risk of seeming to bind that fidelity which a disciple of Christ owes to the law of indissolubility clearly stated by Him, to a civil law which forbade divorce. It is not under the constraint of a civil law, but by virtue of their conscience and faith, and freely in love, that a Christian couple must remain faithful to one another for life.

Such a debate could have offered a unique opportunity for the Church to state clearly Christ's law for Christians without trying to impose it under constraint of a civil law on citizens not professing our faith.

To sum up, the ambiguity of this vote has contributed to disturbing consciences because many people believed it was a question of admitting divorce for Christians or not. This is the way, for example, the NO majority has been interpreted by the press in

France: as a 'defeat' for the church, as the desire of Christians to reject from now on the law on the indissolubility of marriage. Now it was not a question of this!

I hope with all my heart that peace will be made between Christians, as they learn to distinguish the political and civil level, in a nation which can no longer call itself a regime of Christendom, from the level of generous communion between Christians in one and the same obedience to Christ, who forbids his disciples to 'put asunder what Christ has joined together'.

This is why, even though I understand your pastoral concern, I could not in any way find it in myself to disapprove of the position which Brother Carlo Carrento has deemed it right in conscience to take before God.

I cannot imagine that in this case it is possible to speak of disobedience to the Church, because the bishops could not bind the conscience of the faithful in a matter which did not depend directly from their episcopal ministry, but concerned a civil law of the State which is basically quite distinct from a law of the Church.

Perhaps such a way of looking at things was contrary to the spirit of the Concordat? But this is another problem!

Please believe, dear parish priest, in my feelings of brotherly union.

René Voillaume
Prior of the Little Brothers

6   EUCHARIST AND CELIBACY

Spello, June 21st 1983

To the Bishop of Foligno
Dear Monsignor,

I think that no one can can testify to the Church better than you, who came to me in Africa for a spiritual retreat in the desert at Béni-Abbès, to the love I bear for the Eucharist.

Down there in land of Father de Foucauld, as here on the slopes of Mount Subasio, my love has grown for adoration of Jesus in the Eucharistic Mystery in a visible and tangible way. Day and night, in the twenty-five hermitages I have organized, young people, priests and married couples take turns in prolonged and silent prayer.

This was the point of departure for my latest book, *I sought and I Found. It is precisely about love for the Holy Eucharist.* And it is precisely because of this love that I have suffered and go on suffering when I see many areas of the world without this Sign of the death and resurrection of Jesus.

I am not raising the question of celibacy or not. I am celibate by vocation and few people have written such words of exaltation and joy as I have at possessing and living out this wonderful charisma which Jesus handed down by his virginal life.

To me the problem is clear and simple. I can say in addition that I have read and meditated upon the texts which the Congregation in its motherly care proposed to me.

The question is a different one and we could give

it the title of one number of the magazine *Concilium*. 'The community has a right to the Eucharist.'

I would be stupid if I were to think of trying to change a centuries-old tradition of the Church about the bond between Celibacy and Eucharist.

I do not feel this way, and I am quite happy when I see many celibates from the Diocese gathered around the Eucharistic Mystery. To me the problem is a missionary one. I travel a lot and I know the different continents. What ought I to think – in love with the Eucharist as I am – when I see little communities in Brazil left for months and months without Jesus in the Eucharist?

This is my problem and this is the only reason why I have intervened on the subject.

There are celibates? Excellent, let us rejoice. There are none? Do theological questions exist which prevent the Church from ordaining married men? That's all there is to it and I am not the only one to think so.

In my writing you might reprimand me for my tone. It is true: you know me. *But it is only the tone and you must defend my good faith.*

Before dying I hope that the Lord will help me be less violent (I have behind me a lot of years of militancy in Catholic Action and . . . that of Pius XII).

May you help me too, Monsignor.

And please express to our Fathers in the Congregation all my affection for them and my admiration for the most fatherly tone in which they have dealt with my problem.

Brother Carlo

Notes

1

This is the first letter written after his departure from Rome on December 8th 1954. The notepaper carries this heading: Prof. Carlo Carretto – Federazione Internazionale della Gioventù Cattolica – via Torre Rossa, 4 Roma. There was an earlier telegram sent from Ventimiglia dated December 9th 1954: 'Crossing the frontier I take you with me. Carlo.'

1 Marseilles-Orano. These were the first two Brotherhoods Carlo came across in Marseilles (France) he was the guest of the Secretariat-Brotherhood in the rue Tapis-Vert, an area of low-life and prostitution. The Brotherhood of Orano (Algeria) (now closed) in the area near the port, was his first contact with the religious life of the Little Brothers of Jesus in Africa.

2 Sister Dolcidia, whom Carlo affectionately called *Dolce*, entered the Institute of the Daughters of Mary Help of Christians in Turin in 1934 after having worked as a book-keeper. She was mistress for novices and postulants to the Congregation, and supervisory secretary, but above all personal secretary to the Mother General (1938–70). See pp. 13–17 and letter 6.

The Carretto family: father Luigi (1879–1971), mother Maria Rovea (1887–1960), sister Paola Emerenziana (1907), sister Dolcidia (1908–86), brother Carlo

(1910–88), Bishop Pietro (1912), Vittorio (1917–19) and Liliana (1925), who married the lawyer Mario Turchi.

2

1 El-Abiodh-Sidi-Cheikh: a plateau (903 m. high) to the south of Orano, an Islamic holy place to which pilgrimages are made to the tomb of the twelfth century marabout (holy man) Sidi Cheikh and his sons.

Its population is poor, partly nomadic and partly settled.

In 1933 an abandoned little old fort became the 'mother house' of a new kind of religious life along the lines laid down by Charles de Foucauld: the Little Brothers of Jesus (*see letter 3*).

2 Poldo and Nino. Leopoldo Saletti and Giovanni Testa were among Carlo's closest friends from his boyhood years at the Salesian Oratory of the Little Cross in Turin. After intense apostolic activity in the diocese and the whole of North Italy during the war years, they followed Carlo to Rome to the central office of the President of the GIAC: Poldo to the Italian Sporting Centre and Nino to the Soldiers Aid Committee (CAM – Comitato Assistenza Militari) and the Catholic Teachers. With Carlo they took part in the foundation of the Brighter Snow Refuge – Rifugio Nive Candidior at Cervinia (1954).

The Salesian Oratory of the Little Cross deserves a note: it was always dear to Carlo, who said on the sixtieth anniversary of its foundation (1924–84):

'. . . I solemnly declare my pride at having sunk my roots into such rich soil as that of the Oratory, where I received a Christian education, without which who knows what would have become of my life?'

3 White Fathers, a name given to the African Missionaries founded in 1868 by Cardinal Charles Lavigerie (1825–92), archbishop of Algeria. Charles de Foucauld and his spiritual family owed them a debt of deep gratitude.

4 Arturo Paoli (1912), a Tuscan priest (1940), was transferred from his own diocese of Lucca to Rome (1949–54) as head-office manager of GIAC (Gioventù Italiana di Azione Cattolica) (Italian Youth for Catholic Action). He too entered (1954) the Little Brothers of Jesus. Today he is living as a Little Brother of the Gospel in Latin America.

C. Arturo Paoli, *Facendo verità*, Gribaudi, Turin 1984.

5 Sister Paola Emerenziana entered the Daughters of Mary Help of Christians in 1929 after a period of employment. From 1931 to 1981 she held various posts in the Congregation such as teacher, novice, mistress, principal and sub-prioress. Nowadays she lives in the Salesian religious house in Roppolo Castello (Vicenza).

3

1 Charles de Foucauld (1858–1916) was born in Strasbourg on September 15th 1858 into a rich and aristocratic family.

He was orphaned while young, and brought up with his sister Maria by his paternal grandfather. He took up a military career, but preferred a life of pleasure and dissolution to study. But in the end pride and a spirit of adventure prevailed and made an exemplary soldier of him.

A danger-filled exploration of Morocco (1883–84) earned him a medal from the Societé de Geographie. A spiritual crisis which had come to a head while amongst Muslims was wisely and kindly dealt with by his cousin Maria de Bondy (1850–1934) and brought him to the confessional of Fr Henry Huvelin (1838–1910) at the church of St Augustine in Paris. After a pilgrimage to the Holy Land (1889) he entered the Trappists (1890–96) and was sent to a poor monastery in Syria, but left it definitively (1897) to live with the Poor Clares at Nazareth a life in imitation of his 'well-beloved brother and Lord Jesus'. Ordained priest (1901) he began his Sarharan journey in Algeria: first Béni-Abbès, then Tamanrasset. He was killed at nightfall on December 1st 1916.

A Viscount of France who made himself into a beggar, a seeker after God in the desert like the ancient Fathers and at the same time in love with humanity as redeemed by Christ's blood, he became a contemplative and prototype of the twentieth-century evangelical missionary.

Cf. Jean-François Six, *Itinerario spirituale die Charles de Foucauld*, Morcelliana, Brescia 1961; Marguerite Castillon du Perron, *Charles de Foucauld*, Jaca Books, Milan 1986.

2 Little Brothers of Jesus, a congregation under papal rule founded in 1933 by René Voillaume. Nowadays it numbers 274 Brothers and 8 novices of 35 nationalities who live in 115 Brotherhoods spread through 44 countries.

3 René Voillaume (1905), a French priest (1929).

He was followed by another four young priests who received a white religious habit from the hands of Cardinal Verdier in the basilica of Montmartre in Paris on September 8th 1933 and so gave birth to a new religious congregation then called, 'The Little Brothers of the Sacred Heart of Jesus.'

4 [*Seeds of the Desert: Legacy of Charles de Faucould*, pub. A. Clarke Books, 1972] *Come loro* by René Voillaume, edizioni Paoline, Roma 1953. This is the Italian translation, edited by Vanna Casara, of *Au coeur des masses*, Cerf, Paris 1950. The Italian edition has been through 11 reprintings, the latest in 1987.

5

1 Béni-Abbès (Algeria), an oasis with thousands of palm and fruit trees and abundant water, about 500 km. from El-Abiodh-Sidi Cheikh.

Here Charles de Foucauld opened his first Brotherhood in 1901. The hermitage and chapel, restored in 1935, are nowadays looked after by the *Little Sisters of Jesus*, a congregation dependent on the Pope and founded in 1939 by the French Little Sister Magdeleine (1898). Currently, 1350 Sisters and 118 young women postulants and novices of 60 nationalities live in 289 communities in 64 countries.

In the same oasis of Béni-Abbès lives a Brotherhood of the *Little Brothers of the Gospel*, a congregation dependent on the local bishop, founded in 1956 by René Voillaume. The 98 Brothers of 13 nationalities live in 30 Brotherhoods in 20 countries. *See letter 7*

It was moreoever at Béni-Abbès that the different Brotherhoods linked to the name of Charles de Foucauld came together to form the *Charles of Jesus (Father de Foucauld) Association*, in order to establish an over-all unity between them while respecting their different vocations.

Cf. *Jesus Caritas*, quarterly magazine of spirituality of the Charles de Foucauld Family, Abbazia di Sassovivo, 06034 Foligno, no. 20, October 1985, 38–41.

6

1 Lili, nickname for Liliana, the youngest sister.

2 Angela Vespa (1887–1969) held various posts in the Institute of the Daughters of Mary Help of Christians, including mother general (1958–69). For fully 31 years Sr Dolcidia Carretto (*see letter 1*) was her faithful, tactful and prudent personal secretary.

Carlo held Mother Angela in great affection as will be shown by some letters to be published in one of the subsequent collections.

Cf. Maria Collino, *Le mani nelle mani di Dio*, Istituto Figlie di Maria Ausiliatrice, Roma 1988.

7

1 Moncrivello (Vicenza). Community of the Daughters of Mary Help of Christians where Sr Paola Emerenziana was principal.

9

1 Pessione (Turin). Novitiate community of the Daughters of Mary Auxiliatrice, now closed.

2 Pietro Carretto (1912), left for Thailand as a Salesian pupil when only 16 years old. He was ordained priest in 1939 and after various jobs in his Congregation was consecrated bishop of Ratburi in 1951. In 1969 he was transferred to the diocese of Surat Thani

– of which he is now the retired bishop – and remained there for 19 years.

10

1 Cittadella Editrice, Assisi, will publish in 1990 the 'Diary' of Carlo Carretto's Novitiate year in El Abiodh (1954–55).

12

1 Berre (France) on the banks of the 'Etang de Berre' about 50 km. from Marseilles. The population was working class, with many emigrants, employed in the large refineries in the area.

The Berre Brotherhood, founded in 1948, has been closed for some years.

15

1 St Remy (France) near Montbard. Farming and working-class population.

The Brotherhood founded there in 1955 has for many years been the postulancy of the Little Brothers of Jesus.

16

1 St Gildas (France), a tiny island off Brittany acquired by the famous doctor Alexis Carrel (1873–1944), who is buried there.

It is a bleak place, reached in the time of the Little Brothers by a sailing boat. The Brotherhood founded in 1956 is now closed. It was the site of a postulancy and a novitiate, but above all it was a place of hermitage.

21

1 The result of an accident which occurred in the Sahara during his novitiate.

22

1 Picture postcard of Genoa, but posted in France.

23

1 The writing is on a French 'carte postale'.

2 Tamanrasset (Algeria). (Carlo often uses the diminutive *Tam*.) This ancient and important village of the southern Sahara is nowadays a 'revolving-door' town with black Africa, full of immigrants from Mali and Niger; it numbers about 30,000 inhabitants.

It is overlooked by the mountains of Hoggar. Charles de Foucauld took up residence here in order to get to know and to help the Tuareg people (*see letter 3*) and here he was killed. (His body now lies in the little cemetery on the edge of the oasis at El-Golea.)

Alongside the Brotherhoods of the Little Brothers of Jesus at Tamanrasset (*see letter 3*) live the Little Sisters of Jesus (*see letter 5*) and the *Little Sisters of the Sacred Heart*, a congregation dependent on the Pope, founded in 1933 by the Belgian Alida Capart-Maicor, Sr Marie-Charles (1885–1961). The 50 Sisters of 8 nationalities live in 22 Communities spread over 10 countries.

26

1 Picture postcard of Algiers.

27

1 Picture postcard of a southern Algerian landscape.

28

1 Assekrem (Algeria) is a plateau (2728 m high.) in the Hoggar massif (300,000 square miles). 480,000 sq. km.

Charles de Foucauld built a hermitage there (1910) with the aim of helping Tuareg on their way through. From 1958 the Little Brothers of Jesus have continued his original presence up there in the form of prayer, work and welcome.

32

1 Maria Donadeo (1923) from Lombardy, a former national and international director of Young Women's Catholic Action, a nun in the Carmel in the Holy Land and now at the Russian Convent, via della Pisana 342, Rome.

34

1 Guido Borra (1896–1981), Salesian missionary from Piedmont, Counsellor to the Salesian Congregation.

2 Ateneo: a reference to the Pontifical Salesian Athenaeum (PAS), located at the time at the Crocetta in Turin (via Caboto) and moved to Rome in 1965.

3 Rebaudengo: The Institute of Arts and Crafts of the Salesian Congregation, and from 1938 to 1958 seat of the Faculty of Philosophy and Theology of the Pontifical Salesian Athenaeum.

4 Nazzareno Camilleri (1906–1973), Maltese Salesian, dean of the Theology Faculty of the PAS, a master of the spiritual life whose cause for beatification is in progress.

Cf. Eugenio Valentini, *don Nazzareno, Camilleri,* LAS, Rome 1979.

5 Discorsi e Radiomessaggi di Sua Santità Pio XII, PUL, Rome 1959, pp. 258–60 and pp. 266–8.

43

1 This was a documentary by RAI – Radio Televisione Italiana: *Fratelli del deserto,* 1958, directed by Fabiano Fabiani.

47

1 Meryem-Ana (Turkey). 9 km. from Ephesus, on the slopes of Mount Solnisso, there is a little chapel known as the house of *Mother Mary.* On the basis of some visions of Caterina Emmerich (1774–1824), a German mystic, some excavations were made and in 1891 the Lazarene Fathers from Smyrna found the supposed house of Mary as seen and described by the visionary.

As a shrine for both Christians and Muslims, it is still nowadays a place of prayer and pilgrimage.

The Brotherhood was present there from 1959 to 1979.

2 Maria Rovea Carretto died in Rome on December 21st 1960; his father Luigi Carretto was to die on September 19th 1972.

48

1 Farlete (Spain): 40 km. from Saragossa; rural population.

The Brotherhood was founded in 1956 as a novitiate and place of hermitage, due to the many caves close to the mountain.

2 Carlo has left notes on this long retreat which ended on September 15th 1961 with his perpetual profession, in which he offered his life 'for the Church and the salvation of people, especially for Italy and for those with whom and for whom I have worked, young children, my friends and those who have responsibilities in the Church.'

49

1 Moncalvo (Asti). The Sisters of Mary Help of Christians had a hostel and workshop here for the female workers of Dr Vicenza's firm Trasformaziioni Tessili (shirts).

50

1 Carlo is referring to a Brotherhood opened on the outskirts of Marseilles at *St Julien*. It consisted of a little farm on which the Brothers were employed in the byres and the fields.

53

1 Isola del Gran Sasso d'Italia (Teramo), a summer villa area and the birthplace of Anna Carlini (1908–73), the Carretto family housemaid.

55

1 St Laurent de Neste (France), a small village between Toulouse and Lourdes. A rural population. The Brotherhood was open for a short time.

56

1 For a number of years the Rome Brotherhood found accommodation in the apartment kindly loaned to them by the accountant Armando Boccia, a former administrator of the GIAC. It was used by the Brothers and Father Prior as a stopover for comings and goings through Rome.

58

1 *Letters from the Desert*, La Scuola, Brescia 1964: thirty editions.
The book has been translated into Greek, Swahili, Indonesian, Portuguese, French, German, Chinese, Dutch, Polish, Spanish and English.

2 *L'Osservatore Romano*, a political/religious daily newspaper, Vatican City, no. 190 of August 16th–17th 1960, p. 4.

3 *Crociata missionaria*, a fortnightly magazine about missionary activity and cooperation. I have been unable to trace the article.

4 *Oggi*, a weekly magazine of politics, current affairs and the arts, Rizzoli, Milan, no. 4, January 24th 1963, p. 25.
5 Luigi Gedda (1902), a doctor, the founder of the Istituto Gregorio Mendel, had various jobs in Italian Catholic Action at a diocesan and national level: the founder of the Società Operaia and the Comitati

Civici. It was he who called upon Carlo to work in the GIAC.

60

1 Pierre-Marie Théas (1894–1977), the French bishop of Montauban (1940–7), translated to the diocese of Tarbes and Lourdes (1947–70).

64

1 Gandhi, *Pensieri*, edited by Rienzo Colla, preface by Primo Mazzolari, La Locusta, Vicenza 1960.

65

1 Letter sent to Mgr Loris Francesco Capovilla, archbishop of Mesembria and former private secretary to John XXIII (1881–1963).

2 Giovanni Battista Montini (1897–1978), former deputy of FUCI (Federazione Universitaria Catholica Italiana – Italian Catholic University Federation) during his Roman service in the Secretariat of State (1923–33).

He was elected archbishop of Milan (1954) and became Pope (1963), taking the name *Paul VI*. He honoured Carlo with his friendship and his advice and presented him with one of his writings on his admission to the Little Brothers of Jesus.

After his election as Pope he continued his gestures of regard and affection towards the Brotherhood and in 1969 invited René Voillaume to preach the spiritual exercises in the Vatican.

Cf. René Voillaume, *Con Gesù nel deserto*, Morcelliana, Brescia 1969.

67

1 Montant (France). As Carlo wrote to Poldo (*see letter 2*) on January 4th 1964: '. . . I have come here to Montant, a retreat house in the Pyrenees run by one of the many Secular Institutes which have sprung up in the last few decades and which thanks to God . . . and to those who have worked better than we have done ourselves with the workers (I'm almost ashamed to write that word and you understand why). It's a poor and simple farmhouse in which brotherly welcome takes the place of all this world's technology and luxury.'

69

1 'La Scuola di Brescia', a publishing house for which Carlo had great regard and to which he felt grateful for what it did for teachers, both through its publications and through the magazine *Scuola italiana moderna*. His links with the publishing house developed and matured through a long and warm friendship with Vittorio Chizzolini (1907–84), a wise and humble apostle of the Italian school.

70

1 Bindua (Cagliari). A mining village of the Miniere di San Giovanni (lead and zinc) of the Pertusola company of Genoa, a branch of the French company of Peñaroia. The first foundation in Italy (1957) of the Little Brothers of the Gospel was due to the foresight of the bishop of Iglesias, Mgr Giovanni Pirastru (1893–1978).

Carlo wrote in his notes: '. . . I'm leaving for Bindua . . . it's my new destination, it's my new life.

After ten years of life abroad, after ten years of life as a Little Brother, I'm coming back to Italy.

A new chapter is beginning for me as a Little Brother of the Gospel (July 2nd 1964, feast of the Visitation).

In the local Church Carlo rediscovered and reaffirmed an old friendship with Mgr Enea Selis (1910), the auxiliary of Iglesias (1964–8).

2 The 'new message' is a reference to the Little Brothers of the Gospel (*see letter 5*) among whom Carlo had spent some time.

In the meantime the female branch, the *Little Sisters of the Gospel*, had also been established; they were founded in 1963 by René Voillaume.

Today the 75 Sisters from 12 nationalities live in 20 Communities spread over 14 countries.

71

1 Bono (Sassari). This was the town where Carlo had his first job as headmaster (1940–2). Here he made himself an educator even outside the school by building a nursery, a cinema, etc.

Since the secretary of the Sassari Fascist Party did not want these works to go under the name of the Fascist Italian Youth (GIL Gioventin Italiana del Littorio), he imprisoned him for several months in Isili (Cagliari).

73

1 *Ciò che conta è amare*, Ave, Rome 1966. Twenty editions and translated into Spanish, Portuguese, French and English.

74

1 Spello (Perugia), a little town at the foot of Mount Subasio between Assisi and Foligno. After a few months of settling in (1965) (*see appendix 2*), the Little Brothers of the Gospel opened (1966) this Brotherhood for formation, prayer, listening to God and to the Brothers, for work in the rural activities of the area and for welcoming whoever wants to share for a period the community life of the Little Brothers.

In over twenty years thousands of people of all ages, believers and not, of various religions, pilgrims and seekers after the Absolute, have knocked on the ever-open door of the Brotherhood or one of its 25 hermitages. Here Carlo made his passage to heaven on the feast of Saint Francis of Assisi, October 4th 1988.

Cf. Giovanna Negrotto Cambiaso, *Le colline della Speranza*, Cittadella Ed., Assisi 1987.

75

1 The experiment of worker priests was the wish of Cardinal Emmanuel Celestine Suhard, archbishop of Paris in 1943; it was suspended by the Holy See in 1954 and permitted again in 1965; it was very important for the Brotherhood of Charles de Foucauld and it is enough to see René Voillaume's letter from Stanleyville on November 9th 1959, in: *Sul cammino degli uomini*, Morcelliana, Brescia 1967.

Cf. *Jesus Caritas*, spirituality quarterly of the Charles de Foucauld Family, Abbazia di Sassovivo, 06034 Foligno, no. 36, October 1989, pp. 74–7.

76

1 The first film of the director Liliana Cavani on 'Francis of Assisi' (1966).

82

1 *Al di là delle cose*, Cittadella Ed., Assisi 1969. Twenty-two editions and translated into Spanish, French, Japanese, German and English.

2 Carlo lived by and strongly recommended litany prayer and for this reason undertook to rework in his charming and homely style the work *Il pellegrino russo*, Cittadella Ed., Assisi 1969. Thirteen editions.
3 No book of this title was published.

83

1 Carlo often wrote his surname, meaning a little cart, like this in the original of this letter and many other times.

86

1 Ermete Scattoloni (1911), a priest of Umbria (1935), who after many years of work in his diocese of Nocera Umbra-Gualdo Tadino, joined the Little Brothers of the Gospel (1968). He now lives in the Brotherhood of Béni-Abbès (Algeria).

90

1 Siro Silvestri (1913), a priest of Liguria (1937), bishop of Foligno (1955–75), apostolic administrator of Assisi (1966–74), of Nocera-Gualdo (1973–4) and bishop of La Spezia-Sarzana-Brugnato since 1975.

He was the one who welcomed the Little Brothers of the Gospel to Spello and gave them fatherly support, especially in moments of difficulty; he encouraged the birth of another branch of the de Foucauld family: the Little Brothers and Sisters of the *Jesus Caritas Community*, which Mgr Giovanni Benedetti (1917), a priest of Umbria (1940), titular bishop of Limata and auxiliary of Perugia (1974–6) and bishop of Foligno (1976) approved definitively in 1987.

2 *Rocca*, fortnightly magazine of Pro Civitate Christiana, Assisi, no. 23, December 1st 1970, pp. 17–19.

96

1 Giovanni Barra (1914–75), a priest of Piedmont (1937), educator, publicist and parish priest. He was a man of intense prayer and great openness; he was a great promoter and tenacious 'backer' of the lines laid down by Vatican Council 11.

Cf. AA. VV. *l giorni di don Barra*, Alzani, Pinerolo 1988.

101

1 In the run-up to the referendum on divorce (Sunday May 12th 1974), Carlo aligned himself with those who upheld the reasons for a NO vote (abrogation of no-divorce law) by way of a prayer published in the Turin daily newspaper *La Stampa* on May 7th 1974. Thousands of pained or indignant protests followed, but an equal number of messages of understanding and great confidence and hope.

103

1 We have not managed to trace this magazine.

104

1 After Carlo's intervention over the referendum, a parish priest of Spello wrote to René Voillaume demanding that he take a stand.

105

1 *Padre mio mi abbandono a te*, Città Nuova, Rome 1975; eight editions and translated into Spanish, German, Portuguese, English, French, Dutch, Polish and Hungarian.

106

1 Later he will write in these terms to Paul VI:

To His Holiness – Vatican City
Most blessed Father,

During the audience granted yesterday to my brother, Mons. Pietro, you expressed anxiety and sorrow concerning me.

This cannot but cause me to take thought because it affects me deeply.

If only you knew how much I have loved you and do love you, your Holiness!

Have I been imprudent?

I could excuse myself saying that I have followed what I was living out in conscience, but I won't do that. When the Father suffers it is better to be silent and to try to understand. And to understand we need to love, and it is that that I am trying to do at this moment so as to remain in the commandment of Jesus.

I ask you for forgiveness, only for forgiveness, without justifying myself.

I return now into my silence, the silence of the

desert that I accepted freely for ten years, and that I want to find again at Spello, so I will be better prepared for my meeting with the Absolute.

I now understand that the things I wanted to say to the Church, for her freedom from the secular world and for her renewed commitment to the evangelical life, I have said badly and with little humility.

Now I want to keep quiet.

And to choose prayer again as my daily work.

And you will be present, because I love you very much; I love you as I did back in our youth when you fired us with enthusiasm as you spoke to us of the mystery of the Church.

May it please you to bless me as I kneel at your feet.

Brother Carlo Carretto

2 *Servitium*, Priory of Sant' Egidio, Sotto il Monte John XXIII, 1974, no. 6 in series II (Nov–Dec): '*The mystery of Peter*'.

The review is mistakenly presented as an expression of the Carmelite Fathers, but the editorship is composed of laity and religious, representing diverse social and ecclesial situations, who congregate around the Priory of Sant' Egidio.

3 Carlo appeals to Cardinal John Henry Newman (1801–1890) and his *Letter to the Duke of Norfolk*, which appeared in Italy with another title, published by Fratelli Bocca, Turin, 1909. A few fragments 'on it never being permissible to act against conscience' appeared in the daily *Il Giorno*, Milan, May 5th 1974, as part of a feature 'Religion and the modern world' edited by Giancarlo Zizola.

The newspaper cutting, together with other significant correspondence for or against his intervention on divorce law, was kept by Carlo in a file on which he had written in large writing: 'But you abide in my peace'.

109

1 For Carlo every book was the last . . . and so he ended up with 17 titles.

2 *The Desert in the City*, Paulists, Rome 1978. Eight editions and it has been translated into Dutch, French, Spanish, Portuguese, Japanese, Croatian, Polish, Danish, Finnish, Afrikaans, Chinese, Korean, English, German.

110

1 Jean-Marie Raimbaud (1924–1989), a French priest (1950) of the White Fathers, bishop of Laghouat in the Algerian Sahara from 1968 until his death. He ordained Carlo a permanent deacon at Béni-Abbès on January 6th 1969.

111

1 Carlo spoke and wrote several times on the question of the priesthood for married men and, as always happened with him, he naturally aroused strong reactions.

The same Congregation for the Doctrine of the Faith, in the person of its Prefect, Cardinal Joseph Ratzinger, wrote to the bishop of Foligno, Mons. Giovanni Benedetti (*see note 1 to letter 90*), in order that Carlo be invited and referred to reading some texts on the question.

To understand better the thought of Carlo on the subject see *I sought and I found* (Cittadella Editions, Assisi/Queriniana, Brescia 1983). Four editions of this book have been published and it has been translated into French, English, Spanish, Dutch, Portuguese, Polish.